Holy Is a Four-Letter Word

Holy Is a Four-Letter Word

How to Live a Holy Life in an Unholy World

CHARLES C. LAKE
and
MATTHEW I. AYARS

WIPF & STOCK · Eugene, Oregon

HOLY IS A FOUR-LETTER WORD
How to Live a Holy Life in an Unholy World

Wipf & Stock
An Imprint of Wipf and Stock Publishers
199 W. 8th Ave., Suite 3
Eugene, OR 97401

www.wipfandstock.com

PAPERBACK ISBN 13: 978-1-4982-8268-0
HARDCOVER ISBN 13: 978-1-4982-8270-3

Manufactured in the U.S.A.   08/03/2016

CONTENTS

INTRODUCTION

As a linguist, I (Matt) spend a lot of time thinking about language and how it works. One of the subdisciplines of linguistic study is *semantics*. Semantics, generally speaking, is the study of *meaning*. A dictionary is a result of semantic study because dictionaries are concerned solely about what words *mean, or signify*. The word *dog*, for example, is a sign that refers to those domesticated, four-legged, furry animals also known as "man's best friend." Easy, right? But what happens when dad comes home after a long, hard day of work, kicks off his new boots and moans, "Boy, my dogs sure are barkin!"? *Dogs*, in this case, means "feet."

This is a perfect exercise in semantics that helps us to see that *a word's meaning is determined by its context*. This example also demonstrates for us that words can have multiple meanings. Dictionaries testify to this. Thorough dictionaries will list more than one meaning for any given word with the most frequent use of the word listed first.

Take the word *trunk* as another example. *Trunk* can signify the storage area of a car (usually found at the back), a chest or box used for dry storage (usually found at the foot of a bed), the base of a tree that connects the branches to the roots, or the nose of an elephant (usually found at the front of an elephant). The first two definitions are obviously related; they both store things. The third and forth are also related in that they are both typically thick and long (physical characteristics). The point is that a single word can mean a variety of related, or unrelated, things (although the variety of meanings are *usually* related in some way).

But what about the word *holy*? What if we were to look up the word *holy* in a dictionary? The *Oxford English Dictionary* (*OED*), which is accepted as the authoritative, and exhaustive, dictionary of the English Language, defines holy as,

> Kept or regarded as inviolate from ordinary use, and appropriated or set apart for religious use or observance; consecrated, dedicated, *sacred*.[1]

This is the most common use of the word. It, like all other words, has other meanings as well, however, it can primarily be understood as a synonym for *sacred*.

At this point, let me point out that there is another use for dictionaries. My wife and I keep a dictionary nearby when playing Scrabble. While playing Scrabble, we're not concerned with what words *mean* (semantics) as much as *how they are spelled* (which is another subdiscipline of linguistics called *orthography*). Dictionaries not only keep a record of meaning, but also correct spelling.

Have you ever noticed that the word *h-o-l-y* has four letters? *Holy* is a four-letter word! *Wikipedia* defines the phrase "four-letter words" as, "referring to a set of English-language words written with four letters which are considered *profane* . . ."[2]

It is quite ironic that *holy* is a four-letter word! The irony is found in the fact that *holy* means the opposite of *profane*. The verb *profane* means, "to treat (something sacred) with irreverence, disrespect, or contempt."[3] In short, *holy*, while having four letters, is an antonym (i.e. opposite) of a "four-letter word."

In light of all of this, Jesus made a habit out of turning things on their head (recapitulation). He would challenge the way people thought by redefining things by their antonyms (opposites). Take *power*, for example. Humans define *power* as "strength", might, and "potency" (among a series of other synonyms). Jesus, however, says power is *weakness, submission,* and *inability*. What? But weakness is the opposite of power!

Furthermore, we have the example of Jesus teaching us that if you want to live, you must die (Matt 10:39); or, if you want to be first, you must be last (Mark 10:34). There is a degree of irony in each of these.

In this same vein of irony, this book sets out to describe the holy life using *four-letter words*. We will speak more to this in a moment.

---

1. *OED* online, s.v. "holy."
2. *Wikipedia*, s.v. "Four-Letter Word."
3. *OED* online, s.v. "profane."

INTRODUCTION

PROFANITY, POSTMODERNITY, AND THE CALL TO HOLINESS

Humans have this bizarre tendency to desecrate the sacred. There is something perverse in the depths of the human heart that despises purity. Undoubtedly, the weight of sin-guilt makes the human heart bitter and resentful toward those who are free from its chains. This reality is manifest in the cultural phenomenon of profanity.

This point is made evident in a variety of profane words in the English language. Have you ever noticed that profane words are rarely more than desecrating the sacred? The words that make us cringe, that are uttered in fierce rage and moments of carnal human passion, are those words that tend to be associated with the pure.

There is something else happening, however, in contemporary Western culture that is more threatening than the desecration of the sacred. There is a recent trend to deny the very existence of anything sacred. That is, in marching in step with postmodernity, the voice of secular humanist culture says, "Everything is the same. There is no sacred and profane; there is no good or bad. Everything, in the end, is relative."[4]

This sort of posture is a greater threat because of its subtlety. At first glance it is not as shocking as profanity, or overtly evil, but evil it is It is, in fact, the source of corruption and decay in the world. This sort of thinking is no different than what we find in Genesis 3 where we read the account of the origin of sin in the world. Adam and Eve, like much of the postmodern Western world, decide on their own that good and evil are *relative*. Yes, God has declared what was right and wrong (it is wrong to eat of the tree), but that is *God's* definition of good and evil. Eve, in being persuaded by the serpent, decides that if God can have his definition of good and evil, then so can she. She sees that the fruit is good even though God has declared that it's not good. This is *moral autonomy*; deciding on one's own what is good and bad. This is the source of death in the world. Leave God to his own self and let him leave me to mine.

This sort of thinking seriously compromises the scriptural call to holiness in the life of the believer. In fact, it eliminates the biblical concept of holiness altogether.

---

4. The self-defeating nature of these propositions simultaneously invalidates them, by the way.

3

The time seems more appropriate than ever to reexamine and reprioritize the importance of holiness in the life of the church. But perhaps we shy away from the concept of *holy* altogether because we are not sure we could ever attain such a level of right living (with the help of the Holy Spirit). It intimidates us. Surely God didn't really mean what he said when he said, "Be holy, as I am holy." Because of our human failures, we do interpretive acrobats to find alternative interpretations to the plain meaning of the text to match what we wish to read. For example, we interpret this to be a hyperbole, or an exaggeration for the sake of the argument. This interpretation loses its validity based on the fact that there are *no* other hyperbolic commands in the Scriptures (that the authors are aware of). Beyond this, to propose that God would command his people to do something they were incapable of would be to question both his justice and his kindness (which are both extensions of his love and holiness). The Father doesn't challenge his children to strive to attain goals that are out of their reach. More than this, the call to holiness is much more a reflection of God's capacity to work in the life of a believer than the human capacity of achievement.

Let us replace our human failures as our framework for biblical interpretation with Christ's victory. Let us stand not in the fallenness of Adam when we read God's commands, but rather in the risenness of Christ! When we do this, we can begin to take the command to be holy seriously.

REDEEMING THE PROFANE: HOLINESS THROUGH FOUR-LETTER WORDS

But how do we live a holy life in a world that is more and more ambiguous on right and wrong with each passing day? It is our contention that the way to be holy can become clearer through the understanding of a series of, yes you guessed it, four-letter words, one negative and then several positive ones.

One of my favorite stories from the gospels is when the leper comes to Jesus for healing (Mark 8). As a rabbi and teacher of the law it was imperative that Jesus not touch lepers. According to the Torah, coming in contact with leprosy made one unclean and ineligible to partake in sacred activity (like teaching the Torah). This means that when Jesus touched the leper in the story he did something very *taboo*.In other words, by touching the leper, he broke social norms in a deep way.

INTRODUCTION

What Jesus' disciples didn't understand, however, was that things that touch Jesus *do not make Jesus unclean.* Much to the contrary, when things or people touch Jesus, they become clean! Jesus redeems that which he comes in contact with. This same principle is true in the story of Jesus' death. When Jesus comes into contact with death, he redeems it. In Jesus, then, death is not a curse, but the way to life. As Christians we can celebrate death, rather than fear it. Thanks be to Jesus!

What is the significance of this for us here? *Jesus wishes to redeem four-letter words* and this book is out to prove it by offering a simple guide to holy living using four-letter words. Each chapter will treat the topic of holiness and how it intersects with our daily living, all centered on a four-letter word.

It is necessary to start with the negative(as was common rabbinic teaching practice during Jesus' day). We need to understand that "sin" is a four-letter word. Obviously, that will need some explanation. We haven't forgotten how to count! Understanding "sin" as a *four-letter word,* we need to move on to the positive with such words as "holy," "full," "pure," "will," "mind," "body," "rest," "life," "sent," and "call"; and we certainly can't forget "love," which in many ways sums up the entire journey.

There is yet another way of clarifying the way to holy living. Paul challenged the Ephesian believers to "address one another in psalms and hymns and spiritual songs" (Eph 5:19). Christians often sing a better theology than they believe or live. That great theology is often contained in the music of the church, which is why each chapter will end with a psalm, hymn or spiritual song. They are included for the reader to have a time of meditation to reflect on the depths of truth they contain in hopes of better understanding what it means to be holy.

Paul admonished Timothy to "give attention to reading [of the Word of God], to exhortation [challenging the people], and to doctrine [the teachings of the church]." He challenged him to "meditate on these things, give yourself wholly to them; that your profiting may appear to all" (1 Tim 4:13–15, KJV). It would do well for all of us to heed that challenge.

Let's begin by making sure we understand our objective . . . *a holy lifestyle.*

1

———

HOLY

...be holy, because I am holy! —Isaiah 35:8

Grandparenting is awesome. Watching our grandsons, Kyle, Cole, and Luke grow has been one of life's greatest joys. Learning to talk is one of the most fascinating stages of a child's development. Learning a new sound each week, one of our grandsons came to the "t" sound. Quickly he picked up words like "toys," "truck," and when we cleaned off the table at a restaurant, "trash."

Our plan was that he would call me "Papaw" and his grandmother "Mamaw." Watching him struggle with her name, my wife said, "I don't care what he calls me as long as it is not a four-letter word." We don't know how he learned it, but all of a sudden he started calling her "Nana."

One of my wife's desires was for her grandson to say her name before mine (a little family rivalry). Soon after she heard him call her "Nana" for the first time, I joined the family at a local restaurant. My wife couldn't wait to tell me he had said her name first. To prove he really could say her name, I asked him what her name was, and he quickly responded, "Trash." Far worse than some four-letter words!

This reminds me of an important part of thinking about holiness, and that is that *holiness is about God first and foremost, and not about us.* Isaiah reminds us of this when he says, "All our righteous acts are like *filthy rags*; we all shrivel up like a leaf, and like the wind our sins sweep us away" (Isa 64:6a, NIV; italics added). After all, the command to be holy is ultimately more about what *God is capable of accomplishing* than about human achievement. In other words, the command to be holy does not speak to human performance, but to God's perfection.

LIVING IN AN UNHOLY WORLD

I (Charles) recently had the A/C repairman at my house. As much as I appreciated his service, it rubbed me a bit that his language was laced with profanity. He didn't know I was a full-time minister and was somewhat embarrassed when he later asked what I did for a living. The casual manner in which he used such strong language is sadly indicative of the growing presence of profanity in the public sector and media.

In October 2011, a *USA Today* headline read, "@$#&!! What are publishers doing?"[1] The subtitle read, "Musicians do it. So does Broadway." The article commented that now more books add profanity to titles, and they sell because of it. "For publishers, 'sell' is a four-letter word. What used to be profane is becoming prevalent—and very profitable."[2]

The article also cited three songs on Billboard's Hot 100 chart with a common four-letter word in the title. A recent Broadway play starring comedic superstar Chris Rock bore the same four-letter word. A recent bestselling book repeats the same word. The book's editor commented to critics, "It's a book for adults who have heard these words. If you don't like it, don't buy it. Books have a lot to compete with these days."

It is not at all uncommon, then, that in a broken and decaying world we have much more exposure to harsh language than language that is pure, lovely, gentle, kind, loving, edifying, up-lifting, and, well . . . holy. Not only this, but also in a broken world, positive language that flows from a healthy and fresh well of sweet, life-giving water, is sometimes considered *taboo*. Eric Metaxas, author of the best-selling biography of Dietrich Bonhoeffer, rightly expresses that "everyone seems to be afraid to say, 'That's wrong,' for fear of being called a prude."[3]

The Bible teaches that a person's words either acquit or condemn him; that the words of our mouths proceed from our hearts. Jesus himself

1. See Donahue, "For Publishers."
2. Ibid.
3. Ibid.

instructs us, "Out of the abundance of the heart the mouth speaks" (Matt 12:34b). The implication here is that profane language deceives its user; it reveals the brokenness out of which profanity flows. What a story *four-letter words* can tell on us.

So then, to orient our thinking about holiness, it's only appropriate that we begin with the character of God himself.

IT ALL BEGINS WITH A HOLY GOD

When the Israelites had crossed the Red Sea and witnessed the great, re-demptive power of God, they sang, "Who is like you, O Lord, among the gods? Who is like you, majestic in holiness, awesome in glorious deeds, doing wonders?" (Exod 15:11). God is different. He is set apart. This is one of the key meanings that must be centrally placed in our thinking about the word *holy*; otherness.

There are many features of God's nature that make him different. In this particular text, the emphasis is God's *otherness in his ability to redeem humanity*. The gods of the ancient Near Eastern pantheon offered false hope. Their gods were just like humans! They lied, cheated, stole, and their future was left to fate. This is diametrically opposed to *Yahweh Elohim*, the God of Abraham, Isaac and Jacob. The God of the patriarchs, unlike the idols of the world, is good, reliable, loving, just, and honest, and his future is left to none. His existence is *independent from all other beings* (the Judeo-Christian doctrine of transcendence). This is one of the reasons why he is called "I Am." It is because he is set apart so that he is able to offer a new reality to his people. He can offer the hope of a *different* future that isn't marked by the fate of death for all. His people are to share in *His life*. They are to be *holy*.

Furthermore, one of the unforgettable features of the story of the prophet's vision in Isaiah 6 is the trifold, "Holy! Holy! Holy!" refrain of the seraphim's worship song (Isa 6:3). This was repeated when John saw the four living creatures in his vision on the Isle of Patmos, "And the four living creatures, each of them with six wings, are full of eyes all around and within, and day and night they never cease to say, 'Holy, holy, holy, is the Lord God Almighty, who was and is and is to come!'" (Rev 4:8).

The Bible throughout attests to the holiness of God. *Holy* is the word that the Bible uses to express all that is distinctive and transcendent in the revealed nature and character of the Creator, all that brings home to us the infinite distance and difference that there is between him and ourselves. *Holiness* in this sense means quite comprehensively, the "Godness" of God, everything about him, which sets him apart from humanity.

He is different, He is set apart.

GOD'S CALL FOR A HOLY PEOPLE

As an extension of his holiness, God calls Israel to be both a *holy people* and a *holy nation* (Exod 19:6a). Israel's story as recorded in the Old Testament, however, is a tragedy. The prophetic literature (as well as the historical books) is centrally characterized by the unifying theme of judgment for a rebellious people. They failed to respond to the call to share in God's nature (more on *calling* as holiness in ch. 12). They were to be set apart, they were to be different from the broken pagan world, and the Torah (the first five books of the Bible) was their handbook for life. Sadly, they rebelled by violating the Torah and fell right into line with the ways of the pagan world around them.

The new covenant was to respond to this tragedy, as promised by the prophets. The call to holiness doesn't change from the Old Testament to the New. What *does* change is that because of universal access to the indwelling of the Holy Spirit (made possible through the substitutionary death of Jesus), the people of God can *truly* respond to his powerful sanctifying work within us based on our faith in Jesus. This means that even today God is seeking to share his nature with us so that we might be made holy, as he is holy. Peter commands his readers, "But as he who called you is holy, you also be holy in all your conduct, since it it written, 'You shall be holy, for I am holy'" (1 Pet 1:15–16).

This means that holy living flows from being dissociated from sinful practices and being devoted to the life of Godlikeness; to be other than.

THE WORD "HOLY" IN THE WORD OF GOD

The Bible speaks of the *holy name* of God. The Scriptures and the Sabbath are also referred to as "holy." Additionally, in Bible times there were *holy places*. God's ways were also called holy. Most important of all, *God is holy*, and he wants us to be holy as well.

That he wants us to be holy is well established in the Scriptures in these phrases:

For I am the Lord your God. Consecrate yourselves therefore, and be holy for I am holy. (Lev 11:44a)

I appeal to you therefore, brothers, by the mercies of God, to present your bodies as a living sacrifice, holy and acceptable to God, which is your spiritual worship. (Rom 12:1)

. . . who saved us and called us to a holy calling, not because of our works but because of his own purpose and grace, which he gave us in Christ Jesus before the ages began . . . (2 Tim 1:9)

. . . but as he who called you is holy, you also be holy in all your conduct, since it is written, "You shall be holy, for I am holy." (1 Pet 1:15–16)

In the Old Testament, the words "holy" and "holiness" occur more than 830 times. The Hebrew word that the ESV translates "holy" is *qadosh*, which means, "holy, sacred, consecrated, set apart as dedicated to God; by extension: pure, innocent, free from impurity; (n.)[as a noun] holy people of God, saints; as a title of God, 'the Holy One' focuses on God as unique, wholly other."[4] In sum, it signifies God's separation from his creation (not spatial, but transcendent) and his spotless character.

When applied to people, it signifies their ceremonial sanctity issuing from appropriate acts of consecration. Occasionally, at a deeper level of significance, it refers to their ethical righteousness. It speaks of separation and consecration; separation from what is common or unclean, consecration to what is sacred and pure.

In the New Testament, the word carries forward and completes the spiritual-ethical aspect of sanctity in the Old Testament. Specifically, it refers to the imparted holiness that comes as the result of a believer's union with Christ.

And because of him you are in Christ Jesus, who became to us wisdom from God, righteousness and sanctification and redemption. (1 Cor 1:30)

Believers, who through the indwelling presence of the Holy Spirit, share Christ's nature and submit to his lordship, possess a moral quality of character and actions. Thus, they are holy in the NT sense.

---

4. Koehler and Baumgartner, *Hebrew and Aramaic Lexicon*, s.v. "qadosh."

But now that you have been set free from sin and have become slaves to God, the fruit you get leads to sanctification and its end, eternal life. (Rom 6:22)

LIVING A HOLY LIFE

But is a life of personal holiness attainable? The psalmist asks, "Who shall ascend the hill of the Lord? And who shall stand in his holy place?" (Ps 24:3). We also find comfort in the words of Jude, "Now to him who is able to keep you from stumbling and to present you blameless before the presence of his glory with great joy . . ." (Jude 24).

When people truly confront the holiness of God, their reaction will be similar to that of Isaiah who said, "Woe is me! For I am lost; for I am a man of unclean lips, and I dwell in the midst of a people of unclean lips; for my eyes have seen the King, the Lord of hosts!" (Isa 6:5). Meditating on his holiness, we become aware not only of our own uncleanness but also the uncleanness of the world around us, just as Isaiah did.

A young man who began confessing that he had committed his life to Christ was asked what evidence he had that Christ truly had accepted his prayer of repentance. His response was simple but yet profound, "For the first time in my life I felt *clean*." Can we even imagine a holy nation, a country that bows before a holy God and holds to a conviction that a basic holiness permeates things and people; a country void of air pollution and sexual immorality; a country that celebrates the sanctity of sex and the joy of treating one another with behavior that honors a holy God?

The Lord commands us to "be holy as I am holy." Is such a life attainable? If so, how is it attained? This is a controversial topic indeed. Let God's Word answer that question for us with four-letter words in the chapters that follow.

SOME QUESTIONS TO CONSIDER

1. What evidences of unholy living do you witness on a daily basis?

2. What do you see or hear that pollutes rather than purifies?

3. Do any of those evidences exist in your lifestyle?

4. Can you even imagine what a holy nation would look like? Try it.

5. Do you really believe that a holy life is possible? How committed are you to living a holy life?

A HYMN FOR MEDITATION: HOLY, HOLY, HOLY, LORD GOD ALMIGHTY

Holy, holy, holy! Lord God Almighty! Early in the morning our song shall rise to Thee; Holy, holy, holy, merciful and mighty! God in Three Persons, blessed Trinity!

Holy, holy, holy! All the saints adore Thee, Casting down their golden crowns around the glassy sea; Cherubim and seraphim falling down before Thee, Which wert, and art, and evermore shalt be.

Holy, holy, holy! Though the darkness hide Thee, Though the eye of sinful man Thy glory may not see; Only Thou art holy; there is none beside Thee, Perfect in power, in love, and purity.

Holy, holy, holy! Lord God Almighty! All Thy works shall praise Thy Name, in earth, and sky, and sea; Holy, holy, holy, merciful and mighty! God in Three Persons, blessed Trinity! And the four beasts had each of them six wings about him; and they were full of eyes within: and they rest not day and night, saying, Holy, holy, holy, Lord God Almighty, which was, and is, and is to come (Rev 4:8).

Reginald Heber (1783–1826) was a Bishop in the Church of England. He wrote the hymn *Holy, Holy, Holy, Lord God Almighty* in 1826 for the celebration of Trinity Sunday. Trinity Sunday celebrates the Christian doctrine of the Trinity; the three-in-one personage of God: the Father, the Son (God incarnate in Jesus Christ) and the Holy Spirit. It is scheduled on the first Sunday after Pentecost in the Western Christian liturgical calendar, and on the Sunday of Pentecost in Eastern Christianity.

After Heber's unexpected death at age forty-three, his wife found the song among some of his writings and passed it on to noted musician John B. Dykes (1823–1876), who composed and arranged the hymn for publication. Dykes composed the tune *Nicaea* for this hymn in 1861. The tune name is a tribute to the First Council of Nicaea, which formalized the doctrine of the Trinity in AD 325.

2

———

SELF

There is no holiness without humility, and indeed, some spiritual masters are
convinced that in the end there is only one threat to holiness: pride—specifically
the pride of self-autonomy and self-dependence.

—Gordon T. Smith, *Call to the Saints*

In 1981 Pat Riley wrote about the downfall of his team, the New York
Knicks, "They failed to become a dynasty because they suffered from
the disease of *me*."[1] There is basically only one hindrance to the living of a
holy life and that obstacle is *sin*, and at the root of sin is human pride, *the
disease of me.*

Sin is the bitter result of pride. It is our unwillingness to be radically
dependent upon God. Pride is the vice from which all others flow. By its
very nature and presence, it not only destroys humility but all other virtues
simultaneously. Sin is essentially the selfishness of the individual in relation
to God and others, and pride is the inordinate assertion of self.

At the fall, recorded in Genesis 3, self took God's rightful place on
the throne and as a result, humanity has struggled with it ever since. In his
book *Paul, Envoy Extraordinaire*, Malcolm Muggeridge, writes:

1. Riley, *Winner Within*, 40.

> It is precisely when you consider the best in man that you see there is in each of us a hard core of pride or self-centeredness which corrupts our best achievements and blights our best experiences.[2]

That corruption flies in the face of any sense of a holy lifestyle. Muggeridge went on to explain some of the ways humanity's self-centeredness expresses itself:

> In the jealousy which spoils our friendships, in the vanity we feel when we have done something pretty good, in the easy conversion of love into lust, in the meanness which makes us depreciate the efforts of other people, in the distortion of our own judgment, our own self-interest, in our fondness for flattery and our resentment of blame, in our self-assertive profession of fine ideals which we never begin to practice.[3]

The word "holy" would never fit in a list of words such as jealousy, vanity, lust, meanness, self-interest, and resentment.

The *self-life* often manifests itself in a secret spirit of pride, love of human praise, stirrings of anger and impatience, self-will, a jealous disposition, and overall selfishness. And selfishness affects the most valuable relationships of our lives.

Selfishness can be blamed as the major enemy of marriage and of love within the family. Selfishness is hypocritical. While falsely appearing to have many benefits, it actually turns the person in upon himself and interferes with healthy self-giving which is the essence of marital love. Selfishness causes significant pain and suffering in marriages and families. It is a major cause of marital anger, permissive parenting, addictive behaviors, infidelity, separation and ultimately divorce. Unless it is addressed, selfishness leads spouses to treat loved ones as objects and not as valuable persons.

Today's cultural view of marriage is radically different than the biblical view. Today, a spouse's responsibility is not to the meeting of the needs of spouse and family but to finding personal fulfillment and happiness in the relationship. Love is defined more in terms of the emotional and erotic rather than the self-giving. Divorce is made easy and the way out appears as a better option than working through the difficulties that selfishness creates. The beautiful reality is that God is much more concerned with our holiness than our happiness.

2. Muggeridge, *Paul: Envoy Extraordinaire*, 147.
3. Ibid.

The Bible, on the other hand, pictures marriage as a union in which each partner lives for the holiness and happiness of the other. If love is defined in self-giving then divorce is not an option. Marriage is sacred and what God has joined together selfishness should not separate.

Selfishness in marriage and family is demonstrated in insensitivity, excessive anger, exaggeration of one's self-importance, a sense of entitlement, unreasonable expectations, manipulation, and the list can go on. If not confronted, selfishness can be the death of a marriage.

BOTTOM OF FORM

When self is in control, *IT'S ALL ABOUT ME!* When the *London Times* asked a number of writers for essays on "What's Wrong with the World?" G. K. Chesterton sent in the shortest and most to-the-point reply: "Dear Sirs: I am. Sincerely yours, G. K. Chesterton."

"In the beginning God . . ." (Gen 1:1a). In the beginning it was to be *all about God*; but that didn't last long.

> So when the woman saw that the tree was good for food, and that it was a delight to the eyes, and that the tree was to be desired to make one wise, she took of its fruit and ate, and she also gave some to her husband who was with her, and he ate. (Gen 3:6)

The nature of sin was defined by John Wesley to be spiritual pride, that which causes a person to set up idols in his own heart, to bow down to them and worship them, to love himself more than he loves God, and to pay honor unto himself, honor which is due to God alone.

In the truest sense of the word, sin is a four-letter word defined by the word S-E-L-F.

HOW DO WE DEAL WITH THE PROBLEM OF SELF

Eugene Peterson, in *The Message*, describes the self-centered life in Romans 8 with gripping terms: "that fateful dilemma; a continuous, low-lying black cloud; a fated lifetime of brutal tyranny" (Rom 8:1–2, *The Message*). He comments on a self-centered life with these thoughts: "Obsession with self is a dead end; focusing on self is opposite of focusing on God; completely absorbed in self ignores God and what He is doing. He calls it the old do-it-yourself life" (Rom 8:5–8, *The Message*).

Paul, however, in Romans 6, teaches that God has provided a remedy. When the Holy Spirit takes control of our lives a new power is in operation. In Christ we find freedom from the bondage of self-centeredness. It is up to us to appropriate God's provision, to allow the Holy Spirit to accomplish his work in our heart. In doing so, we must experience God on his terms and not our own.

When Jesus offered the invitation for people to follow him, his invitation included the words: "If anyone would come after me, let him deny himself and take up his cross daily and follow me" (Luke 9:23). Self-denial is the denial of the false self, not the self in totality. A healthy view of self includes appropriate self-respect and even self-love. It is proper to have a good feeling about our human nature. We may not deserve to be saved, but we are worth saving. There is a pride that is not sinful.

Dietrich Bonhoeffer once wrote, "When Christ calls a man, he bids him come and die."[4] No one says it better than Paul when, in the letter to the Galatians, he speaks of being "crucified with Christ" using the word "crucified" three times in Galatians:

> I have been crucified with Christ. It is no longer I who live, but Christ who lives in me. And the life I now live in the flesh I live by faith in the Son of God, who loved me and gave himself for me. (Gal 2:20)

To be "crucified to self" means to have a change of relation to one's self; to cease to be under its supervision. To be in Christ is to forfeit one's self-given right to be under one's own supervision. This is accomplished by identification by faith in Christ's death and resurrection and is, therefore, *tied to a historical reality*. The verb is in the perfect tense and points to the once-and-for-all-ness of one's crucifixion with continuing results into the present. It implies a new kind of life, not ego-centered but Christ-centered, one motivated and guided by his sacrificial love.

CRUCIFYING THE SINFUL NATURE

Crucifying the sinful nature is precisely what Paul is talking about when he says, "And those who belong to Christ Jesus have crucified the flesh with its passions and desires" (Gal 5:24).

---

4. Bonhoeffer, *Cost of Discipleship*, 7.

The crucifixion of the sinful nature refers to a crucifixion that defeats the carnal, delivers the human, and prioritizes the spiritual. It settles the question of priorities and mastery and infers a daily renunciation of sin, saying "no" to the sins of the flesh.

CRUCIFYING THE WORLD'S INFLUENCE

"But far be it from me to boast except in the cross of our Lord Jesus Christ, by which the world has been crucified to me, and I to the world" (Gal 6:14). Being "crucified to the world" means eliminating any reason for boasting in self and causes the world to lose its hold and appeal. The songwriter said it well when he wrote, "The things of earth grow strangely dim in the light of his glory and grace."

Freedom from a Self-Centered Life: Dying to Self is a small brochure that includes selections from the writing of William Law, edited by Andrew Murray. William Law was an Anglican priest who lost his position at Emmanuel College (Cambridge) when his conscience would not allow him to take the required oath of allegiance to the first Hanoverian monarch, George I. Thereafter, Law continued as a simple priest and when that too became impossible without the required oath, Law taught privately, and wrote extensively. His personal integrity, as well as mystical and theological writing greatly influenced the evangelical movement of his day and remain in print today. On the cover are these words:

> Not I, but Christ
> Lord, bend that proud and stiff-necked I
> Help me to bow the neck and die,
> Beholding him on Calvary,
> Who bowed his head for me.

The key to living a holy, Christ-centered life can be found at Calvary and just before Calvary, the garden of Gethsemane. A fitting prayer for any person who is seeking life to its fullest is:

> Oh, to be saved from myself, dear Lord,
> Oh, to be lost in Thee;
> Oh, that it might be no more I,
> But Christ that lives in me.

Pauline had to be one of the most selfish individuals her peers had ever encountered. Her life motto was, "It's all about me!" In any group setting,

Pauline had to have her way or else she would pout. In some situations, her pouting would turn to anger and volatile outbursts.

Her selfishness manifested itself in the life of her family. Early in life she found it difficult to share her toys with her siblings. She was prone to temper tantrums when she didn't get her way. She made life miserable for her parents, brothers and sister.

Her selfishness carried over into her teen years. Although a very popular girl around her peers due to her looks, athletic ability, and scholarship, she negatively flavored every occasion her peers sought to enjoy. They had to go where she wanted to go, when she wanted to go and by what means she wanted to travel. Pauline was totally insensitive to the desires and feelings of others.

In her freshman year of college she encountered some members of a Christian group who reached out to her with compassion. They refused to allow her self-centeredness to distract them from sharing their faith with her and praying for her to see herself as others saw her.

A member of the group was reading the classic *The Cost of Discipleship*, by Dietrich Bonhoeffer. Over coffee in the student lounge, the girl shared with the group that profound statement in the book, "When Christ calls a man, he bids him come and die." Although Pauline didn't have a clue what that meant, she couldn't escape those words. They haunted her for days after she first heard them.

While sleepless one night, she determined to explore further what Bonhoeffer meant by the statement. She sought the girl who had initially shared the statement and asked her to explain. Thus, Pauline began a journey to not only understand and experience a relationship with Christ but also understand what it meant to be a true follower of Christ.

To the group she shared her newfound discovery, "I am crucified with Christ," she exclaimed, "nevertheless, I live and yet not I, but Christ lives in me." Her life changed remarkably and her family noticed it the most. When home for a weekend, she prepared to return to campus. Her parent's last words to her were, "We don't know what's happened to you but we sure love the *new you*." Later, Pauline rejoiced in sharing her newfound faith with her family.

In 2008 Mark Sayers was leading an Australian church in Melbourne known for being culturally engaged and missionally inventive. A challenging question, asked of him by his fourteen-year-old daughter, precipitated a change in his view of Christian leadership. In an interview with *Christianity Today* in October of 2014, Sayers commented,

> The way I had measured success was wrong. It wasn't about retweets, book sales, and buzz. It was about dying to self in public. It was not about building a career or a name. It was about operating out of complete dependency upon God. He was far more interested in what he wanted to do in me than in what I was doing. So I became focused on passing the baton to others, stepping out of the way so others could flourish. I learned that Christian leadership in a shallow age had to depend on him. I learned that when God leads you through suffering and trial, and when you press into him, you return with spiritual authority.[5]

DYING TO SELF

1. When you are forgotten, neglected or purposely ignored, and you don't sulk or hurt with the insult or oversight, but your heart is happy, that is dying to self.

2. When your good is spoken of as evil, your wishes are crossed, your advice disregarded, your opinions ridiculed, and you refuse to let anger rise in your heart, or even defend yourself, but take it all in patient, loving silence, that is dying to self.

3. When you never care to refer to yourself in conversation, record your own good works, itch for commendation; when you are comfortable being unknown, that is dying to self.

4. When you can see your brother prosper and have his needs met, and can honestly rejoice with him in spirit and feel no envy nor jealousy, though your own needs are far greater and you are in desperate circumstances, that is dying to self.

5. When you can receive correction and reproof from someone of less stature than yourself and can humbly submit inwardly as well as outwardly, finding no resentment or bitterness rising up in your heart, that is dying to self.

5. Dyck, "Rising Above the Spectacle," 52.

Jealousy, vanity, lust, meanness, anger, self-interest, and resentment all find their root in selfishness. Think of all the pain and sorrow that could be averted if the *disease of me* was eliminated from the relationships of our lives. Christ has provided a way of escape. It challenges us to consider the option.

SOME QUESTIONS TO CONSIDER

1. In the garden of Gethsemane Jesus prayed, "Not my will but thine be done." Is that a prayer that marks your life?

2. Can you honestly say, "It is not about me. It's all about him. I, too, am crucified with Christ"?

3. How do you operate in a group? How willing are you to give into the wishes of the group especially when they make choices that are not your preference?

A HYMN FOR MEDITATION: SO I SEND YOU

So send I you to labor unrewarded, to serve unpaid, unloved, unsought, unknown, to bear rebuke, to suffer scorn and scoffing—so send I you to toil for me alone.

So send I you to bind the bruised and broken, O'er wandering souls to work, to weep, to wake, to bear the burdens of a world a-weary—so send I you to suffer for my sake. So send I you to loneliness and longing, with heart a hungering for the loved and known, forsaking home and kindred, friend and dear one—so send I you to know my love alone.

So send I you to leave your life's ambition, to die to dear desire, self-will resign, to labor long, and love where men revile you—so send I you to lose your life in mine. So send I you to hearts made hard by hatred, to eyes made blind because they will not see, to spend, tho' it be blood, to spend and spare not—so send I you to taste of Calvary.

As the Father hath sent me, so send I you.

Margaret Clarkson was born in 1915 in a small city in Saskatchewan, Canada. She was born into an unhappy home, was bed-bound with juvenile arthritis when she was three, and suffered migraines and vomiting. Pain was a constant companion, but she was able to attend school. She was trained as a schoolteacher and became an acclaimed author and hymn writer. During her early years she taught in a remote mining camp where she experienced mental, cultural and spiritual loneliness. She lacked spiritual fellowship as the churches were liberal in doctrine and evangelical Christians were hard to find.

While meditating on Scripture one evening, she read John 20:21, "As the Father hath sent me, so send I you." God used those words to speak to her about her circumstances. She believed for the first time that she was where God had sent her. As a result she wrote a poem that later was set to music. The song speaks clearly of the painful sacrifice some are called to make for the cause of Christ.

Some years later, she viewed her song with a different eye. She did not deny the truth of the song she had written but came to believe there was another side to the coin. Not only are there sometimes painful sacrifices to make, there are also boundless joys to experience. Meditation on the contrast between the two songs can stir the heart.

Most Christians will never be called on to live a life of sacrifice as described in Clarkson's song, but Spirit-filled Christians who are truly *crucified with Christ* will certainly be willing should that be the desire of God for their lives.

3

FULL

You know him, for he dwells with you and will be in you —John 14:17

Do not get drunk with wine ... but be filled with the Spirit. — Ephesians 5:18

Kevin began his own business soon after graduating from university. He soon experienced the favor of God upon his work. Business exceeded expectations and profits were more than he ever dreamed.

In a service at his church, he heard the pastor preaching on stewardship and felt the need to become a bit more generous in his giving than he had been before. He added a few extra dollars the following week and felt pretty good about himself for being so unselfish. However, as he prayed about his giving, God confronted him in a way he had not anticipated.

God was not wanting *more*; he was asking for *all*. Initially, Kevin argued with God. After all, what he had accumulated was due to a lot of hard work on his part. Surely he had the right to do with his money what he chose to do. But God was relentless.

At the close of a service at a men's retreat God's persistence was quite evident to Kevin. He knew what he needed to do but was reluctant. Toward the end of an invitation to surrender all to God, Kevin knew it was time for him to unconditionally place everything he had under God's control.

The following days, months, and years Kevin knew an inner peace and joy in knowing that all that he possessed belonged to God and God was blessing him beyond measure. He experienced a power in his life that manifested itself in a greater victory over temptation and a deeper understanding of God's Word and how to apply it to his life. He knew a deeper joy than he had ever known before.

Unexpectedly, however, the economy hit the skids and his industry was particularly hit hard. Soon he found his business suffering and the profits dwindling. Some of his investments had turned sour.

Kevin never compromised his surrender. However, in time, he saw his business go into bankruptcy and the bank issued a foreclosure on his home. Never would he have dreamed of the circumstances in which he found himself. Soon after another company employed him, and he and his family were living in a house half the size of their previous one. Yet in the midst of it all, Kevin was at peace. Frequently he uttered the words of Job, "The Lord gave and the Lord has taken away; blessed be the name of the Lord" (Job 1:21). Kevin never blamed God for his losses. He maintained his trust in God's provision and never once went without his and his family's basic needs.

The economy is back on the rise and the possibility exists that Kevin might regain ownership of his previous business. His wife and family are content in their present home and with anticipation they wait to see what the future holds.

CONTROL, NOT QUANTITY

For those of an older generation, driving into a filling station and telling the attendant, "Fill'er up!" was a common experience. Self-service has now replaced that action and the patron must get out of his car and *fill it up* by himself. In the majority of cases *to fill* implies quantity. We seldom use the word any other way. However, when Paul used the word in Ephesians 5:18, he was not referring to quantity but control.

Being filled does not denote quantity but control; one personality possessing another. In Acts 5:3 Peter asks, "Ananias, why has Satan filled your heart to lie to the Holy Spirit . . . ?" In the same chapter, verse 17, the Sadducees were said to be "filled with jealousy" of the disciples that they had the arrested. In Romans 1:29 we read, "They were filled with all manner of unrighteousness, evil, covetousness, malice. They are filled of envy, murder, strife, deceit, maliciousness . . ." Satan and his evil qualities are not liquid to be poured into anyone, but can fill and master one who yields himself to him.

Someone once asked a friend of Dwight L. Moody, "Does Dr. Moody have a monopoly on the Holy Spirit?" The reply, "No, but the Holy Spirit has a monopoly on Mr. Moody."

God's original purpose in creation was that the Holy Spirit dwell in each person. Humanity's sin evicted the Holy Spirit from the human heart. Redemption through Christ restores man to a proper relationship with God, wherein the Holy Spirit takes up residence within a person's heart (Rom 8:9).

God desires to indwell and fully possess the life of a redeemed man. People must be cleansed of an inner nature of polluted and perverted desires and affections, a self-centeredness inherited from Adam. Such a cleansing results in the personal indwelling and control of man's heart by the Holy Spirit.

Early in his career, Kevin found himself somewhat full of himself, thinking mostly of his merited success and his right to control all that he had earned. At that men's retreat, however, he surrendered control and was *filled with the Holy Spirit*.

Thus, Paul could admonish the Galatian believers, "If we live by the Spirit, let us also keep in step with the Spirit" (Gal 5:25).

CHARACTERISTICS OF A HOLY LIFE

Our text infers five characteristics of a Spirit-filled life.

1. **Imperative**. Be filled with the Spirit (Eph 5:18)

2. **Exclusive**. The Holy Spirit can only occupy a person's heart when he does so without an inward rival.

3. **Personal**. A human personality is filled with a divine personality. One person filled with, dominated and completely controlled by another.

4. **Progressive**. Marks a beginning, not a conclusion. The present imperative tense of the verb "be filled" implies that the experience of receiving the fullness of the Spirit is not a once-for-all experience. The Christian is to leave his life open to be filled constantly and repeatedly by the divine Spirit.

5. **Purity is not maturity**. Obtainment is not attainment. A literal translation of Paul's admonition can read "be you being filled."

6. **Intoxicating**. "Do not get drunk on wine, which leads to excess." Christians know a better way than wine to be lifted above the depression and monotony of life. They know a better way to remove self-centeredness; to quicken thought, word, and action than by the use of intoxicants. A better way is by being intoxicated with the Holy Spirit.

It is interesting to note the response of non-believing observers on the day of Pentecost. The text reads, "But others mocking said, 'They are filled with new wine.'" To which Peter responded, "These men are not drunk, as you suppose . . ." (Acts 2:13, 15).

God wills that his people be personally indwelt by the Holy Spirit. Christ promised the Indweller whose presence was fully realized on the day of Pentecost. The Holy Spirit was to be to the believer all that Christ was and more. He is unlimited by bodily form and is omnipresent, the constant companion in the believer's life. Thus, the Spirit's indwelling is the internal experience of the believer of the presence of Christ's spiritual nature; God's permanent gift to all believers "to be with you forever" (John 14:16).

In a sense, Paul was speaking of spiritual intoxication. When a man is intoxicated with strong drink, he experiences exhilaration; *excessively he* experiences uncontrolled action, lack of self-control, and wastefulness. But when he is *intoxicated* with the Holy Spirit, he experiences joy and being under the control of the Holy Spirit maximizes his full potential.

TO YIELD OR NOT TO YIELD

The word "control" congers up negative thoughts in the minds of most people today. We don't want to be controlled by someone other than ourselves. The *OED* defines control as, "The fact of controlling, or of checking and directing action; the function or power of directing and regulating; domination, command, sway."[1]

In the late 1960s, an era when great stress was laid on the principle of "doing one's own thing" and letting others do the same, the term "control freak" was coined. It was a derogatory term for people who attempt to dictate how everything around them should be done. No one wants to be known as a control freak, let alone be controlled by one.

1. *OED* online, s.v. "control."

The role of the Trinity in guiding the life of a devoted follower of Christ greatly tempers the issue. The psalmist says of the Lord, his shepherd, "He leads me beside still waters" (Ps 23:2b). Solomon said of the fear of the Lord, "The fear of the Lord leads to life" (Prov 19:23). Isaiah speaks of the Sovereign Lord, "He will tend his flock like a shepherd; he will gather the lambs in his arms; he will carry them in his bosom, and gently lead those that are with young" (Isa 40:11). John, using the same analogy, writes of Christ, "To him the gatekeeper opens. The sheep hear his voice, and he calls his own sheep by name and leads them out. When he has brought out all his own, he goes before them, and the sheep follow him, for they know his voice" (John 10:3–4). Paul adds an awesome touch, "But thanks be to God, who in Christ always leads us in triumphal procession, and through us spreads the fragrance of the knowledge of him everywhere" (2 Cor 2:14).

The above passages make a great argument for choosing to live a life controlled by the by the Spirit. Everyone is controlled by something or someone. We can choose to be controlled by alcohol, pleasure, fortune, fame, or we can choose to control our own lives. God has an agenda for each of us. How much better that we let him be our guide? Putting our lives under his control places us in position for fulfilling the very purpose for which we are *set aside* by him.

Such was true of the early followers of Christ.

- For he will be great before the Lord. And he must not drink wine or strong drink, and he will be filled with the Holy Spirit, even from his mother's womb. (Luke 1:15)

- Then Peter, filled with the Holy Spirit, said to them, "Rulers of the people and elders . . ." (Acts 4:8)

- But he [Stephen], full of the Holy Spirit, gazed into heaven and saw the glory of God, and Jesus standing at the right hand of God. (Acts 7:55)

- For he [Barnabas] was a good man, full of the Holy Spirit and of faith. And a great many people were added to the Lord. (Acts 11:24)

- But Saul, who was also called Paul, filled with the Holy Spirit, looked intently at him . . . (Acts 13:9)

- And the disciples were filled with joy and with the Holy Spirit. (Acts 13:52)

When I (Charles) was a young boy, my grandparents' home was a fun place to visit, especially in the fall. Harvest time took Grandpa to the small garden in his back field to harvest the fruit of his summer-long toil. Corn and beans were canned. Beets were picked. Cucumbers were turned into pickles and cabbage became sauerkraut. I found it fascinating to watch the processes that were involved in making it all happen.

Cabbage was turned into sauerkraut using large crocks. During the winter potatoes were often stored in them. Thus, in order for them to be used, grandpa would first empty them and wash them to make them clean. Then they were ready to be filled with the shredded cabbage. Once filled with all the necessary ingredients, weights were placed on the top of the crocks. They were then covered and were then in use.

The verbs of that process have always fascinated me; "emptied," "cleansed," "filled," and then "used." Sounds familiar to the process believers have to go through in order to be filled by the Spirit and then used by God. *Emptied* of self, *cleansed,* and *filled* with the Holy Spirit, people are ready to be used.

To ask the Lord to fill you with his Spirit is a noble prayer, but only as it is asked in response to willingness to totally yield the control of one's life to his lordship.

ARE NOT ALL BELIEVERS FILLED WITH THE SPIRIT?

But are not all believers filled with the Spirit? Is there not a marked difference between being *baptized in the Spirit* and *being filled with the Spirit,* a distinction that many believers fail to discover?

All believers have been baptized in the Spirit. Ephesians 4:5 tells us that there is only "one Lord, one faith, and one baptism . . ." First Corinthians 12:12–13 also explains that,

> for just as the body is one and has many members, and all the members of the body, though many, are one body, so it is with Christ. For in one Spirit we were all baptized into one body—Jews or Greeks, slaves or free—and all were made to drink of one Spirit.

Galatians 3:26–27 further states, "For ye are all the children of God by faith in Christ Jesus. For as many of you as have been baptized into Christ have put on Christ" (KJV).

Christian baptism is symbolic of the baptism of the Holy Spirit and refers to an internal working of God's divine Spirit in the heart of the believer. On the basis of the above scriptures, it can be concluded that all believers have been "baptized in the Spirit" as the baptism of the Spirit and conversion are synonymous.

But not all believers have been *filled* with the Spirit, and nowhere is that better exemplified than in the life of the Corinthian believers. Just as there were carnal Christians in the church then, there are yet today. There are carnal believers in today's church who know the witness of the Spirit but do not know his fullness, have been freed from sin's penalty but have not been delivered from sin's power, have appropriated by faith the forgiveness of their sins but have not appropriated his deliverance from a sinful nature. They live after the flesh not after the Spirit and know Jesus as Savior but do not acknowledge him as Lord.

The greatest need in most churches today is for Spirit-filled leadership and Spirit-filled fellowship. Congregations that emphasize and experience the indwelling fullness of the Spirit are congregations who put the needs of others before their own and experience a unity that many other churches would covet.

HOW DOES ONE EXPERIENCE THE FULLNESS OF THE SPIRIT? THE CONTRIBUTION OF CAMPUS CRUSADE FOR CHRIST

CCFC (today known as Cru) was founded in 1951 on the campus of the University of California, Los Angeles, by William R. "Bill" Bright (1921–2003) as a Christian ministry to university students. Dr. Bright is well known for his book *The Four Spiritual Laws: Have You Made the Wonderful Discovery of the Spirit-Filled Life,* and the production of the *Jesus Film* (1979).

In 1996, Dr. Bright was awarded the $1.1 million Templeton Prize for Progress in Religion and donated the money to promote the spiritual benefits of fasting and prayer. In 2001 he stepped down as leader of the organization and died in 2003. The ministry he established continues as a viable ministry yet today.

The Four Spiritual Laws begins with the positive affirmation: "Everyday can be an exciting adventure for the Christian who knows the reality of being filled with the Holy Spirit and who lives constantly, moment by moment, under his gracious direction."

What believer wouldn't be enticed with such a statement?

The booklet goes on to describe three kinds of people: (1) the natural person (someone who has not received Christ); (2) the spiritual person (one who is directed and empowered by the Holy Spirit); and (3) the carnal person (one who has received Christ but lives in defeat because he is trying to live the Christian life in his own strength). The trichotomy is based on 1 Corinthians 2.

The booklet goes on to affirm that "God has provided for us an abundant and fruitful Christian life," and asks, "Why is it that most Christians are not experiencing the abundant life?" The answer given: carnal Christians cannot experience the abundant and fruitful Christian life. The carnal person trusts in his own efforts to live the Christian life. The pamphlet suggests that the only solution to this problem is that Jesus promised the abundant and fruitful life as the result of being filled (directed and empowered) by the Holy Spirit. The Spirit-filled life is the Christ-directed life by which Christ lives his life in and through us in the power of the Holy Spirit (John 15).

"How, then, can one be filled with the Holy Spirit?" is the booklet's final question. The answer? "We are filled by the Holy Spirit by faith." Then the conditions are listed: You can appropriate the filling of the Holy Spirit right now if you:

- Sincerely desire to be directed and empowered by the Holy Spirit. (Matt 5:6; John 7:37–39)

- Confess your sins. By faith, thank God that he has forgiven all of your sins—past, present and future—because Christ died for you. (Col 2:13–15; 1 John 1; 2:1–3; Heb 10:1–17)

- Present every area of your life to God. (Rom 12:1–2)

- By faith claim the fullness of the Holy Spirit, according to: (1) His Command: Be filled with the Spirit. "And do not get drunk with wine, for that is debauchery, but be filled with the Spirit" (Eph 5:18); (2) His Promise: He will always answer when we pray according to his will. "And this is the confidence that we have toward him, that if we ask anything according to his will he hears us. And if we know that he hears us in whatever we ask, we know that we have the requests that we have asked of him." (1 John 5:14–15)

A suggested prayer is offered:

> Dear Father, I need you. I acknowledge that I have been directing my own life and that, as a result, I have sinned against you. I thank you that you have forgiven my sins through Christ's death on the cross for me. I now invite Christ to again take his place on the

throne of my life. Fill me with the Holy Spirit as you commanded me to be filled, and as you promised in your Word that you would do if I asked in faith. I now thank you for directing my life and for filling me with the Holy Spirit.

In the conclusion of the pamphlet suggestions are given as to how to walk in the Spirit. Two relevant and practical instructions are given:

> If you become aware of an area of your life (an attitude or an action) that is displeasing to the Lord, even though you are walking with Him and sincerely desiring to serve Him . . . claim His love and forgiveness by faith and continue to have fellowship with Him. If you retake the throne of your life through sin — a definite act of disobedience—recommit yourself to His Lordship and continue to follow Him.

God alone knows how many college students and adults have followed the direction given by Dr. Bright's writing. Many have followed suite and have made that amazing discover of being controlled by the Holy Spirit.

SOME QUESTIONS TO CONSIDER

1. Can you communicate to someone else the difference between being baptized and being filled with the Holy Spirit?

2. Can you witness to the fullness of the Spirit in your life?

3. What evidences have you seen in your life as you live in total dependency on him?

A HYMN FOR MEDITATION: BREATH ON ME, BREATH OF GOD

Breathe On Me, Breathe of God
Breathe on me, breath of God, Fill me with life anew,
That I may love what Thou dost love, And do what Thou wouldst do.
Breathe on me, breath of God, Until my heart is pure,
Until with Thee I will one will, To do and to endure.
Breathe on me, Breath of God, Till I am wholly Thine, Until this
    earthly part of me
Glows with Thy fire divine.

Breathe on me, Breath of God, So shall I never die, But live with
Thee the perfect life, Of Thine eternity.

The simplicity of this profound hymn belies the education and knowledge of its author, Edwin Hatch (1835–1889). Educated at Pembroke College, Oxford, Hatch ministered in an Anglican parish in the slums of east
London before accepting a position at Trinity College in Quebec where he
taught classics.

After serving as Rector of Quebec High School, he returned to Oxford to become the vice-principal of St. Mary's Hall and took several posts
including the Bampton Lecturer, Reader in Ecclesiastical History, and the
Hibbert Lecturer.

In spite of Hatch's scholarship, his one remaining hymn reflects both
a profound simplicity and a deep knowledge of the Scriptures. The hymn
draws largely from John 20:21–22, following John's account of the resurrection, for its inspiration: "Jesus said to them again, 'Peace be with you. As
the Father has sent me, even, so send I you.' And when he had said this, he
breathed on them, and said to them, 'Receive the Holy Spirit'" (RSV).

This passage in John echoes with Genesis 2:7 where "the Lord God
formed the man of dust from the ground and breathed into his nostrils the
breath of life, and the man became a living creature."

The author invokes the Holy Spirit to come into his life and transform
it. Using the first-person perspective throughout the hymn adds to the
hymn's power as the singer seeks the breath of God (Gen 2:7) as a source
for renewal.

4

PURE

And God, who knows the heart, bore witness to them, by giving them the Holy Spirit just as he did to us, and he made no distinction between us and them, having cleansed their hearts by faith. —Acts 15:8–9

Blessed are the pure in heart, for they shall see God. —Matthew 5:8

The salvation of Christ is a salvation from the smallest tendency or leaning to sin. It is deliverance into the pure air of God's ways of thinking and feeling. It is a salvation that makes the heart pure with the will and the choice of the heart to be pure. To such a heart, sin is disgusting. —George MacDonald, *Heart of George MacDonald*

Archibald Joseph Cronin (1896–1981) was a Scottish novelist and physician. In his autobiography, *Adventures in Two Worlds*, he tells of a district nurse who for twenty years, single-handedly, served a ten-mile district. "I marveled at her patience, her fortitude and cheerfulness. She was never too tired at night to rise for an urgent call. Her salary was most inadequate, and late one night, after a particularly strenuous day, I ventured to protest to her, 'Nurse, why don't you make them pay you more? God knows you are worth it.' 'If God knows I'm worth it,' she answered, 'that's all that matters to me.'" No one ever questioned the purity of her motives.

Take a moment and think about all the ways in which the word "pure" can be applied. We can talk about pure water, purebred animals, sounds can be pure, gold can be pure, and the list goes on. When something is pure, it is unmixed, or uncontaminated. Purity is different than simply *clean*. Something that is pure is without contamination in both *seen* and *unseen* dimensions. So what does purity have to do with living a holy lifestyle? Purity and holy living, in fact, go hand-in-hand.

There are three ways in which they align. The first has to do with the sinful being decontaminated or purified from sin, the second with having an unmixed will, and the third with living a pure life.

PURIFICATION FROM SIN AND THE SACRIFICIAL SYSTEM

Psalm 51 is a favorite psalm. It tells the story of the gracious, reconciling, and purifying work of God in response to King David's humility and repentance. As a repentance psalm it illustrates the biblical metaphor of sin as defilement. David's words of repentance bring the metaphor to life:

> Wash me thoroughly from my iniquity, and cleanse me from my sin! (v. 2)

> Purge me with hyssop, and I shall be clean; wash me, and I shall be whiter than snow. (v. 7)

> Hide your face from my sins, and blot out all my iniquities. Create in me a clean heart, O God, and renew a right spirit within me. (vv. 9–10)

The words "wash" (2x), "cleanse," "purge," "clean" (2x), and "blot out" correspond to purity. Seven times the psalm uses the purity metaphor in connection to sin. The consequential dynamic of sin that the contamination metaphor symbolizes is *guilt*. *To be unclean is to be guilty*. To be impure, or contaminated, is to be marked as worthy of blame.

The rituals and procedures for purification from sin that are detailed in the sacrificial system of the Old Testament serve as an object lesson which makes guilt, the unseen consequence of sin, tangible. The symbol of the sacrificial system served not only the purpose of helping God's people get a firm grasp on the guilt of sin, but also God's gracious rescue plan that centered in forgiveness through the cross.

The sacrificial system detailed that those who were guilty of sin would be declared innocent through a sin offering, which included taking the life of an animal. Through death alone, the guilt of sin could be lifted. The sprinkling of blood cleansed the sinner from defilement (Isa 52:15).Thanks to the justice of God, sin must be punished.

Once a year on the Day of Atonement, the impurity, or guilt of the sins of the people, was reversed with the sprinkling of blood on the ark of the covenant. This activity meant presenting before the God of Israel (represented by the ark of the covenant), the life of the animal (represented in the blood) so that their sins could be forgiven. Thankfully, by God's grace, his people were given the option of offering another in their place so that the consequence of sin, which defiles, could be lifted from them and placed onto a substitute. In this activity worshippers were made clean. Worshippers were alleviated from the guilt of their sin. The death of the animal symbolized the consequence of sin (death) being transferred from the worshipper to the animal.

The point here is that sin-guilt is punishable by death. On the other side of the coin, to be clean or pure is to be innocent, or righteous. *To be holy is to be declared not guilty, to be pure, clean, innocent, and righteous.* This status can only come through sacrifice. As Jesus offers his life as a sacrifice for sin, our guilt is forgiven and we are declared clean, pure, innocent, and righteous. We are cleansed from the contamination of sin. It is through Jesus and Jesus alone that people are made pure.

To be holy is to be pure, to be fully free from the guilt of sin.

PURITY OF HEART

Another sense in which purity and holy living come together is at the place of the heart. Here, the heart represents the will, where our desires originate. To talk about a pure heart is to say something about our intentions, our desires, and our will. How does this work?

A young seminarian wrestled with the concept of a pure heart. One day Katherine picked up a small book written in 1968 by Dr. James R. Bishop, entitled *The Spirit of Christ in Human Relationships*. In his opening chapter, Dr. Bishop tells the following two stories that, after Katherine had read them, the concept became explicitly clear.

A devoted mother was tireless in nursing her sick child. Night and day she watched over the little form, seeking in every way to bring it back to life and health, but her strength was waning. The night was dark, and the light in the room was dim. She gave the child what she thought was its healing medicine; but, too late, she discovered it to be poison! The child soon died, and the mother was grief-stricken beyond words. Friends flocked in to console her. Nobody blamed her. Her intention was perfect, but her judgment was faulty.

A godly man was obliged to spend long periods of time away from home. Returning on one occasion to his family, he went out into his vegetable garden to pull weeds from a patch of beans. One of his small children, a little girl four or five years of age, came out to "help daddy." While he was on his knees moving down a row of beans, the little darling worked along behind him calling out from time to time, "I'se a helpin' you, Daddy." The affectionate father would call back, "All right, darling," and go on with his work. Reaching the end of the row, he turned about, and what did he see? His willing little helper had come along behind him and instead of pulling weeds, she had pulled up all the beans! What did he do? Become angry and gave the child a good beating? No! He gathered her in his arms, gave her a good hug to show his gratitude for her good intentions to "help daddy" and carried her to the house where she would be kept from giving him further "help." The child had a perfect heart, but a faulty head. Her motive was faultless but not her service.

To Katherine the concept not only became clear but also an object of personal pursuit. She desired a pure heart. Prayerfully she pursued God's cleansing in her life, motives that projected God's unconditional love to others. She later described the new revelation as a milestone in her spiritual journey.

Something that is pure is unblended, unmixed. There is only one element, not several. Pure gold is just gold, and nothing else. To have a pure heart, is to have pure, unblended, and fixed will. And what is that will? To love and obey God first and foremost with no competing desires. That is what John Wesley meant when he talked about Christian perfection. He talked about a will, a heart that is completely devoted to God. Purity of heart is when we have completely abandoned all our selfish desires and have aligned our desires with Christ and his will alone. This means having a pure heart, to abide in Christ and no where else.

Once again, we find this idea as well in Psalm 51. David pled for cleansing, for forgiveness, but also to "create in me a new heart, O God, and renew a right spirit within me" (51:10). David is asking that he not only be purified from the sins he has committed, but also that God would align his heart so as to protect against future potential sins. David is asking God to make his heart pure, unblended, unmixed, and fixed on doing the will of God alone.

It is through the empowerment of the Holy Spirit that we can be pure in heart, be alleviated from the guilt of sin, and have a will that is fully devoted to doing the will of God.

PURITY OF LIFE

The psalmist asked, "How can a young man keep his way pure?," and then answered his own question, "By guarding it according to your word" (Ps 119:9). One would certainly believe that the psalmist thought it possible to be pure in one's lifestyle.

Paul would have joined him in that conviction. Writing to the Corinthians in his second letter, he shares a concern,

> For I feel a divine jealousy for you, since I betrothed you to one husband, to present you as a pure virgin to Christ. But I am afraid that as the serpent deceived Eve by his cunning, your thoughts will be led astray from a sincere and pure devotion to Christ. For if someone comes and proclaims another Jesus than the one we proclaimed, or if you receive a different spirit from the one you received, or if you accept a different gospel from the one you accepted, you put up with it readily enough. (2 Cor 11:2–4)

Paul believed the Philippians could keep their minds pure by focusing on pure ideas. "Finally, brothers, whatever is true, whatever is honorable, whatever is just, whatever is pure, whatever is lovely, whatever is commendable, if there is any excellence, if there is anything worthy of praise, think about these things" (Phil 4:8). The discipline of the mind may not eliminate Satan's temptations to think impure thoughts, but discipline and the grace of God can enable one to refuse to allow those thoughts to linger. The old adage is true, "You can't keep the birds from flying over your head but you can keep them from building a nest in your hair."

Sexual purity is paramount in the teaching of scripture "Let marriage be held in honor among all, and let the marriage bed be undefiled, for God will judge the sexually immoral and adulterous" (Heb 13:4). Jean Vanier, founder of *l'Arche*, an international federation of communities for people with developmental disabilities, believes that purity is a sign of hope, an effort to bring personal order into a disordered world. Purity can be sought as a celibate single person or as a married person. Either state involves loneliness and sometimes anguish as well as hope. 'Blessed are the pure in heart, for they will see God.' Note the extent of the promise: not that they will find complete sexual fulfillment and solve all loneliness, but that they will see God.[1]

The book of Proverbs also asked, "Who can say, 'I have made my heart pure; I am clean from my sin?'" (20:9). Obviously, no one can say, "I am without sin," but one can have a pure heart and a pure mind through the enabling power of the Holy Spirit who indwells him.

- Create in me a clean heart, O God, and renew a right spirit within me. (Ps 51:10)

- Who shall ascend the hill of the Lord? And who shall stand in his holy place? He who has clean hands and a pure heart, who does not lift up his soul to what is false and does not swear deceitfully. (Ps 24:3–4)

- What agreement has the temple of God with idols? For we are the temple of the living God; as God said, "I will make my dwelling among them and walk among them, and I will be their God, and they shall be my people. Therefore, go out from their midst, and be separate from them, says the Lord and touch no unclean thing; then I will welcome you, and I will be a father to you, and you shall be sons and daughters to me, says the Lord Almighty." Since we have these promises, beloved, let us cleanse ourselves from every defilement of body and spirit, bringing holiness to completion in the fear of God. (2 Cor 6:16–7:1)

The words "pig iron," "ladle," and "ingot" are generally not familiar words to the average person, but they were to Dean. His father worked more than forty-five years in a steel mill and each of those words played a very important part in explaining the process by which steel was made, a process which he was allowed to observe on one occasion when the employees were allowed to bring their sons to see where they worked.

His father worked at the blast furnace where the actual process of making steel began. Pig iron is one of the ingredients in making steel. Ladles were the fire brick-lined containers in which the molten steel was poured and the ingots were the large blocks of steel sent to the rolling mill to be rolled into sheets of steel for the making of automobiles.

1. Yancey, quoting Vanier, in *Rumors of Another World*, 87.

Few things about his father's job ever fascinated Dean more than seeing the resultant molten steels after all the impurities were removed by the heat of the fire in the furnace. A small dipper was often used to test the product being made before it was sent from the furnace to be rolled into sheets. He would never forget a comment made by his dad, "After the fire in the furnace, the molten metal is so pure that you can actually see your face reflected on its surface."

One could pray that the hearts of believers be so pure that the reflection of the face of Jesus could be seen in them. Sometimes it takes the fire of life's crisis to burn away the dross but it does not have to be. He is more willing to purify the hearts of men than we are to allow him to do so. Let the Scriptures speak for themselves and dare to pray the prayer of the psalmist, "Create in me a pure heart, O God" (NIV).

LIVING A LIFE THAT IS PURE

So how does one live a pure lifestyle in an impure world? Begin by knowing that your body is the temple of the Holy Spirit. As a follower of Christ, know that in him, his blood cleanses you from all sin. "What God has made clean, do not call common" (Acts 10:15). With a will to do his will serve him from a pure heart reflecting pure motives.

"Therefore go out from their midst, and be separate from them, says the Lord, and touch no unclean thing; then I will welcome you" (2 Cor 6:17). Living a separated lifestyle is not a popular theme in today's society. Finding balance between liberty and license, a Christ-followers are challenged to work out their own salvation with fear and trembling (Phil 2:12). Adjusting habits and thoughts stand among the greatest challenges.

Habits

"Working out your own salvation" negates accepting a list of do's and don'ts from someone else. We don't need lists but biblical principles that can guide us and indeed be helpful. Consider a few:

- Romans 14 speaks to us of our responsibility to our *weaker brother*. We should do nothing that might cause a brother to stumble.

- 1 Corinthians 5 warns us of keeping fellowship with those who live a life of hypocrisy. We should not associate with anyone who calls himself a brother but is sexually immoral or greedy, or an idolater, or a slanderer, a drunkard or a swindler.

- 1 Corinthians 6 addresses addictive behaviors. We should not allow ourselves to be mastered by anything while honoring God with our body.

The world ultimately respects the believer who stands for his convictions and lives a life exemplary of Christ. We must keep guard that nothing in our lives will ever detract from our usefulness and effectiveness for the kingdom.

Thoughts

"We take captive every thought to make it obedient to Christ" (2 Cor 10:5b NIV). *The Message* paraphrases it succinctly, "fitting every loose thought and emotion and impulse into the structure of life shaped by Christ."

Paul simplified it by instructing the Philippians, "Whatever is true, noble, right, pure, lovely, admirable—if anything is excellent or praiseworthy—think about such things" (Phil 4:8, NIV). Again, *The Message* clarifies by paraphrasing, "I'd say you'll do best by filling your minds and meditating on things true, noble, reputable, authentic, compelling, gracious—the best, not the worst, the beautiful, not the ugly, things to praise, not things to curse."

An antidote for impure thoughts is to let God put a song in your heart. We will explore this issue further in chapter 6.

Let us purify ourselves from everything that contaminates body and spirit, perfecting holiness out of reverence for God (2 Cor 7:1). Living a life of personal purity is possible. Don't let the enemy tell you differently.

SOME QUESTIONS TO CONSIDER

1. If someone were to ask you what it meant to have a pure heart, how would you answer?

2. Are you willing to take a serious look at your motives? Why do you do what you do? For whose praise and glory do you live?

3. Would you be daring enough to pray the prayer of the psalmist, asking God to give you a pure heart? Ask the Lord to convict you of any unclean habit in your life.

A GOSPEL SONG FOR MEDITATION: A REFINER'S FIRE

Brian Robert Doerksen is a Canadian songwriter and worship leader. For many years Doerksen was part of the Vineyard Churches as well as Vineyard Music Group. In that context he was extremely influential in the area of contemporary Christian worship music. He was a featured worship leader on many Vineyard worship CDs and also taught extensively on worship leading and song writing. Brian's worship recordings are known for their high production values and quality songwriting.

Among his more notable songs are "Refiner's Fire" (1990) and "Come, Now Is the Time to Worship" (1998). More recently Brian Doerksen has been producing worship music through Integrity's Hosanna Music. Brian received a Gospel Music Association Dove Award in 2003, only the second Canadian to be so honored.

A REFINER'S FIRE

Purify my heart, Let me be as gold and precious silver
Purify my heart, Let me be as gold, pure gold
Refiner's fire, My heart's one desire, Is to be holy
Set apart for You, Lord, I choose to be holy
Set apart for You, my Master, Ready to do Your will
Purify my heart, Cleanse me from within, And make me holy
Purify my heart, Cleanse me from my sin, Deep within

He will sit as a refiner and purifier of silver, and he will purify the sons of Levi and refine them like gold and silver, and they will bring offerings in righteousness to the Lord. (Mal 3:3)

Refining in the Bible was of both liquids and metals. The processes were very different. For liquids the objective was that of straining or filtering. For metals, it was that of melting. In the course of time, refining came to be used of gold or other precious metals to bring them to a refined or pure state. The refining resulted in the separation of the dross from the pure ore, which was effected by reducing the metal to a fluid state by the application of heat and by the aid of solvents. The solvent amalgamated with the dross, permitting the extraction of the unadulterated, pure metal. The instruments required were a crucible or furnace, and a bellows or blowpipe. The workman sat at his work to watch the process and let the metal run off at the proper moment.

Have you ever experienced the *refiner's fire?* What were the circumstances? How was the timing? Was the *workman* always keeping watch? What were the results? Ponder these things in your heart.

5

WILL

But in your hearts honor Christ the Lord as holy . . . —1 Peter 3:15

Each day offers numerous opportunities to either grow in grace or to allow the effects of the fall to spread in our hearts and our relationships with others. Free will gives us an essential choice: we can willfully make a decision to allow sin to progress in our lives by giving into some form of temptation, or we can willingly surrender to the power of the Holy Spirit and take the way of escape God offers. We do not have to yield to temptation.

A fascinating phrase in the KJV account of the Prodigal Son is, "and when he came to himself" (Luke 15:17, KJV). The phrase can be found only one additional time in the Bible, "Then Peter came to himself" (Acts 12:11). Applying a little logic, one can come to some significant conclusions.

If the prodigal and Peter both "came to themselves," what were they before they did so? They were something other than themselves. The prodigal was in a pigpen and Peter was in prison. The prodigal was as sin had made him; he was less than himself. Peter was as the Holy Spirit had empowered him; he was much more than himself. When the prodigal willed to act on his new awareness and when Peter willed to obey God's angel, both experienced a divine moment in their lives.

Daily we have that choice, to yield to temptation and sin or to yield our wills to the will of the Father and allow the Holy Spirit to take control. A holy life is a life surrendered to the will of the Father. A commitment to live a holy life is a commitment to die to a self-centered existence and to live a Christ-centered one.

William Booth, founder of the Salvation Army, once said, "The greatness of a man's power is in the measure of his surrender." To the world, the word "surrender" is a sign of weakness, but to the follower of Christ it is the secret of his strength.

Few churchgoing Americans today would be incapable of reciting the Lord's Prayer, but how many really understand what they are praying? To pray, "Your kingdom come, your will be done, on earth as it is in heaven" (Matt 6:10), is indeed a sobering request. If sincerely prayed, the petition simply re-echoes the prayer of our Master in the Garden of Gethsemane, "Father, if you are willing, remove this cup from me. Nevertheless, not my will, but yours, be done" (Luke 22:42).

To pray, "If it be your will," is not a cop-out! In 1 John 5:14 the promise is to us, "ask anything according to his will." Prayer is a mighty tool, not for getting our will done in heaven, but for getting God's will done in earth. We have no right to ask God to do anything against his will. Few but sobering are the illustrations of prayers God answered against his will.

First Samuel 9 is a sad episode in Israel's history. Discouraged by the corruption and perversion of Samuel's sons whom he had appointed as judges, the Israelites requested that Samuel appoint a king to lead them so they could be as other nations. The request displeased Samuel. When he talked it over with God, God responded, "They have not rejected you, but they have rejected me as their king."

Samuel was instructed to listen to the people, yet warn them of the consequences should they persist in their request. "But the people refused to listen. No, they said. We want a king over us." God agreed to give them what they had requested, and Israel suffered the consequences of failing to surrender to the lordship of God their king.

As our (Charles) daughters reached adulthood, there was a possibility that one would end up going to a mission field. Confronting the issue of being separated by thousands of miles from your daughter, her husband and family is a daunting challenge to any parent. I count my wealth in family (not dollars) and I consider myself the richest man in the world. Apart from Christ, my family means everything to me.

My wife's response was immediate and duplicated mine. We would rather see our daughter and her family separated from us by many miles and be in the will of God than have her live next door and be out of the will of God. Why would anyone want the Lord to give them that which was not in his will? To do so is to assume that we are wiser than God and know better than he what is best for us.

At the beginning of the remarkable ministry of Christ (John 4) Jesus ministered to the Samaritan woman, giving her to drink of living water. When the disciples returned from having acquired food, they failed to understand why he refused to share in their meal. "I have food to eat that you know nothing about," was his response. Immediately they thought that someone had brought in food in their absence but not so. "My food is to do the will of him who sent me and to finish his work."

Toward the end of his ministry, Jesus, in the Upper Room was able to pray with his disciples (John 17) and say to his Father, "I have brought you glory on earth by completing the work you gave me to do." He had accomplished the total will of the Father. When James and John asked to sit on the right and left hand of Christ in his kingdom, he asked them, "Can you drink the cup I drink or be baptized with the baptism I am baptized with?" Jesus was not referring to a literal cup. He was referring to the same cup he talked about with his Father in the garden of Gethsemane, "If it be possible, let this cup pass from me." The cup was the will of the Father. To *drink it* was to surrender to it and that he did.

Although the living of a holy lifestyle is a progressive journey, it begins, as it were, in Gethsemane, a place where a Christ-follower prays the prayer of Jesus and to the best of his ability and knowledge surrenders his will to the will of his Father. It means a willingness to do God's will in regard to one's possessions (Luke 14:33), the object of one's affections, and one's future plans and ambitions (14:26).

To desire to know and do God's will places one in great company. Hear the psalmist pray, "Teach me to do your will, for you are my God! Let your good Spirit lead me on level ground!" (143:10). When Paul prayed for the churches, his frequent request was that they "understand what the will of the Lord is" (Eph 5:17). That people can, with God's enabling, control their will is attested in 1 Corinthians 7:37 when it speaks of a man who "settles the matter in his own mind, who being under no compulsion has control over his own will, makes up his mind," what to do and what not to do (NIV).

People can reject God's will just as Jerusalem did in Matthew 23:37. The words are filled with pathos:

> O Jerusalem, Jerusalem, the city that kills the prophets and stones those who are sent to it! How often would I have gathered your children together as a hen gathers her brood under her wings, and you were not willing!

Saul of Tarsus knew the pain of rebellion against the will of God. Several manuscripts add to Christ's words to Saul in Acts 9:4, "Saul, Saul, why do you persecute me? It is hard for you to kick against the pricks" (KJV). In a very picturesque statement, God likened Saul's rebellion to an ox kicking against the long goad held in the hand of his master when he refused to follow his master's commands. A believer pursuing a holy life is a believer surrendered to the will of the Father, ready to take *the cup* and drink it regardless of the cost.

A day must come in our lives, as definite as the day of our conversion, when we give up all right to ourselves and submit to the absolute Lordship of Christ, surrendering ourselves, our loved ones, our possessions, our present, and our future. It's the day we surrender control of our lives to him and we begin to enjoy the freedom that is ours in Christ.

Ben was a student at a Christian university. Ben's family considered him to be a strong-willed child. Ben wrestled with always having to have his way. He found it hard to bring his life into conformity to the will of Christ and equally difficult to bring himself under the authority of those whom God had placed in authority over him. He had even lost a summer job because of his lack of obedient response to a foreman on his job.

A message he heard one morning in chapel, however, was not on trying but on surrendering oneself totally to Christ to allow him to change and transform his life.

Ben's prayerful response was to surrender his all to Christ, but to no avail. It seemed as if God was not listening. At that moment, the speaker shared a comment and illustration that was "made to order" for Ben.

> Someone responding to Christ's call to surrender is making no progress. You're trying to do business with God on your terms, not his. You're asking God to show you your future and if you like it, you're in for the ride. God doesn't do business that way. He gives you a contract on a blank sheet of paper and asks you to sign your name. He'll sign his and then take the rest of your life filling out

the details. He'll take responsibility for your direction and will be there to guide you.

The message resonated with Ben and he prayerfully "signed" his name to the contract. That day Ben began a new journey. He began to see his life transformed in ways that he had always desired but never imagined possible.

God had started a transformation in his life that he never dreamt could exist. Ben even felt led to go to the foreman on his summer job and apologize for his belligerence. He asked his parents to forgive him for the pain he had caused them when he had refused to obey their request. Little had he guessed that the implications of his decision that day to surrender his will to the will of God would be so far reaching in his life.

The battle of the will is one of the greatest, if not the greatest battle a person will ever face. Surrender is not easy, nor painless. Rebellion, however, is more painful. It is hard to kick against the goads.

The *battlefields of my own making* find their root in our human selfishness. Selfishness is placing concern with oneself or one's own interests above the well-being or interests of others. It is demanding my will not his.

A believer, reading in 1 Corinthians 7, might find the content somewhat irrelevant to where he is in his life and, in doing so, miss a very relevant, transferable principle found in verse 37.

1. NIV—But the man who has settled the matter in his own mind

2. KJV—He that standeth steadfast in his heart

3. NIV—who is under no compulsion

4. KJV—having no necessity

5. NIV—but has control over his own will

6. KJV—hath power over his own will

7. NIV—and has made up his mind

8. KJV—hath so decreed in his heart . . . this man also does the right thing.

Three significant observations to apply to one's life are:

1. The heart is the center from which decisions are made.

2. Individuals have the power to control their own decision-making.

3. Good decisions are objective, independent of pleasing others.

4. Decisions can become settled convictions. I have decided to follow Jesus! No turning back, no turning back! My will is to do his will. A call to standing steadfast.

Such steadfastness is beautifully demonstrated in the lives of many who have preceded us.

1. **Joseph.** "He is not greater in this house than I am, nor has he kept back anything from me except you, because you are his wife. How then can I do this great wickedness and sin against God?" (Gen 39:9)

2. **Daniel.** "But Daniel resolved that he would not defile himself with the king's food, or with the wine that he drank. Therefore he asked the chief of the eunuchs to allow him not to defile himself." (Dan 1:8)

3. **Shadrach, Meshach and Abednego.** "'But if not, be it known to you, O king, that we will not serve your gods or worship the golden image that you have set up.' Then Nebuchadnezzar was filled with fury, and the expression of his face was changed against Shadrach, Meshach, and Abednego. He ordered the furnace heated seven times more than it was usually heated." (Dan 3:18–19)

4. **Polycarp.** "Eighty and six years have I served Him, and He has done me no wrong. How then can I blaspheme my King and my Savior? Let me be; He who gives me strength to endure the flames will give me strength not to flinch at the stake, without our making sure of it with nails."[1]

SOME QUESTIONS TO CONSIDER

1. Is it possible for a believer to know Jesus as Savior without knowing Jesus as Lord? Can you say with conviction that Jesus is Lord of your life?

2. Do you consider yourself objective when making decisions? Do you hold strong convictions that hold you steadfast when making them?

3. What has been the most difficult area of your life to surrender to his will and control?

1. *Martyrdom of Polycarp*, translated by J. B. Lightfoot [9.3]

A GOSPEL SONG FOR MEDITATION: I AM THINE, O LORD

Fanny B. Crosby

While much could be written about the life of one of the most famous hymn writers of all time, *Wikipedia* shares this edited paragraph, which has relevance to our study.

> While not identified publicly with the American holiness movement of the second half of the 19th century, and despite having left no record of an experience of entire sanctification, Crosby was a fellow traveler of the Wesleyan holiness movement, including in her circle of friends some of the prominent members of the movement and attending Wesleyan/Holiness meetings. For example, Crosby was a friend of Walter and Phoebe Palmer, "the mother of the holiness movement," and "arguably the most influential female theologian in Christian history," and their daughter Phoebe Knapp, with whom she wrote "Blessed Assurance," often visiting the Methodist campgrounds at Ocean Grove, New Jersey, as their guest. For many years (from at least 1877 until at least 1897), Crosby vacationed each summer at Ocean Grove, where she would speak in the Great Auditorium and hold receptions in her cottage to meet her admirers.[2]

In 1877 Crosby met William J. Kirkpatrick, one of the most prolific composers of gospel song tunes, and "the most prominent publisher in the Wesleyan/Holiness Movement,"[3] with whom she wrote many hymns. Some of her hymns reflected her Wesleyan beliefs, including her call to consecrated Christian living in "I Am Thine, O Lord" (1875).

Fanny Crosby, although physically blind, had spiritual insight beyond the expectations of many. Insight reflected in her treasured hymns and gospel songs was exceptional.

I Am Thine, O Lord

> I am Thine, O Lord, I have heard Thy voice, And it told Thy love to me; But I long to rise in the arms of faith, And be closer drawn to Thee.

2. *Wikipedia*, s.v. "Fanny Crosby."
3. Ibid.

Refrain: Draw me nearer, nearer blessed Lord, To the cross where Thou hast died; Draw me nearer, nearer, nearer blessed Lord, To Thy precious, bleeding side.

Consecrate me now to Thy service, Lord, By the power of grace divine; Let my soul look up with a steadfast hope, And my will be lost in Thine.

Oh, the pure delight of a single hour, That before Thy throne I spend, When I kneel in prayer, and with Thee, my God, I commune as friend with friend!

There are depths of love that I cannot know, Till I cross the narrow sea; There are heights of joy that I may not reach, Till I rest in peace with Thee.

6

MIND

Do not be conformed to this world, but be transformed by the renewal of your mind, that by testing you may discern what is the will of God, what is good and acceptable and perfect. — Romans 12:2

Whatever gets your attention gets you. —E. Stanley Jones[1]

The youth pastor was stunned. His premier male leader in the youth group was praying at the altar of the church following a public invitation. Surely, he was there praying for someone else. When Tim refused to share with anyone but him, the youth pastor took him aside where they could talk freely.

"How can I be of help?" he asked.

Much to his surprise he heard the teen reply, "I have the dirtiest mind in town!" The youth pastor was shocked. Never would he have guessed that Tim wrestled with such a problem.

"It all began when I found some pornography hidden at home by my step-dad. At first, I found it repulsive but found myself returning to it again and again. I began to notice how it was affecting my relationships

1. A quote with which he began each message in a series at the Spiritual Emphasis Week at Asbury College in 1961.

with others. My girlfriend broke up with me because she said I was going too far when I expressed my affection for her. She said she could no longer respect me."

"Around the guys," he confessed, "I found myself being entertained by their off-colored humor which before I had simply ignored while finding it distasteful. I had never understood how strongly your thought life could affect your behavior."

The youth pastor was in possession of a discipleship program that was designed for men with addictive behaviors. Week after week, he met with Tim holding him accountable for his thought life. "I guess this is what you would call the renewing of your mind," shared Tim after having a daily quiet time in the twelfth chapter of Romans.

In time, Tim was able to share the freedom that was his from yielding his mind as a servant of righteousness. He constantly reminded himself that you can't keep the birds from flying over your head but you can keep them from building a nest in your hair. Weekly, he would proudly say to his pastor, "I had a great week and could offer my thoughts to God as a token of praise to him."

THE DARKENED MIND

The Scriptures use a variety of metaphors to conceptualize the problem of sin. One of those metaphors is the corruption, debasement, or darkening of the mind. Jesus himself demonstrates the difference between the mind of God and the mind of humanity with these famous words of rebuke to Peter, "For you are not setting you mind on the things of God, but on the things of man" (Mark 8:33). Paul describes those who are not in Christ as having a corrupt, or debased mind in Romans 1:28, "And since they did not see fit to acknowledge God, God gave them up to a debased mind to do what ought not to be done."

Jesus makes it clear that sinful humanity does not think the way that God thinks. The mind of humanity has tragically deviated from God's original design. God created humanity with a mind that resembled his own, but tragically, that was lost through disobedience.

Thankfully, the Gospel and the message of holy living is the story of hope; hope for the renewal of the mind. The message of a holy lifestyle teaches us that we are, in fact, and with the help of the Holy Spirit, *able to think differently*. The message proclaims that the mind once broken and corrupt can be healed and restored. Through the powerful presence of the Holy Spirit, our minds are illuminated to a new reality. A commitment to a holy lifestyle is a commitment to the renewing of the mind.

So how does this work? What does it mean to have a renewed mind and how does the renewed mind relate to holy living?

PAUL, THE WORK OF JESUS AND THE RENEWED MIND

Paul, more than all of the other New Testament writers, talks about those who are in Christ as having renewed minds. To the believers in Rome Paul says, "Do not be conformed to this world, but be transformed by the renewal of your mind, that by testing you may discern what is the will of God, what is good and acceptable and perfect" (Rom 12:12). So what did Paul mean, exactly, when he talked about the "renewal of the mind" for those who embrace the work of Christ?

Once we personally accept God's forgiveness for our sins, sin, death, shame, guilt, doubt, and fear, no longer reign over us and over our minds. Without the forgiveness of sins, every thought is held captive to the power of sin and death. Thankfully, because Jesus put sin to death along with the full gambit of consequences for sin, we have the opportunity for new life.

The past has been put to death and Jesus has ushered in the new day with the forgiveness of sins and the resurrection of the body. Jesus and life are now the point of reference for every thought. This is precisely what Paul means when he says, "We destroy arguments and every lofty opinion raised against the knowledge of God, and take every thought captive to obey Christ" (2 Cor. 10:5).

Because of Jesus, sin is no longer our master. Jesus is our master. Sin, shame, guilt, fear and doubt no longer sit on the throne of our minds; it is now Jesus who is rightfully enthroned. The dark shadow that was once cast over our minds because of sin, death, and guilt is now driven out through the forgiveness of sins. The new day has come. Jesus, through the cross and resurrection, broke the power of sin over his people.

HOLY LIVING AND A RENEWED MIND

So how does holy living link up to a renewed mind? What does having a renewed mind through the forgiveness of sins have to do with being "set apart," or "different"? First and foremost, now that our minds can see clearly thanks to the forgiveness of sins, we are able to live with a heavenly wisdom and polished clarity. The way in which we perceive and understand circumstances in life affects the decisions we make. Now that the shadow of death is gone, we are illuminated by the Holy Spirit so that we can analyze circumstances with God's perspective. Those who are in Christ by faith will make very different decisions than those who are in the world. In fact, Paul says that to those that are perishing the decisions that Christians make to be foolish.

In addressing this, Paul says, "Where is the one who is wise? Where is the scribe? Where is the debater of this age? Has not God made foolish the wisdom of the world? . . . It pleased God through the folly of what we preach to save those who believe" (1 Cor 1:20–21). The mind of those in Christ is so different than those who are not in Christ that those who are not in Christ can't even begin to understand the Christian frame of reference for thought and wisdom. In this way, the renewed mind is holy.

HOLY LIVING AND A LOVING PERSPECTIVE

There's yet another way that the renewed mind connects to a holy life. A holy lifestyle is not only defined as being "other," but as being love. This means that the renewed mind, with its new frame-of-reference being grace, love, and forgiveness perceives the world and individuals in an entirely new way. When we look at the world and people through the lens of sin we count them as threatening, ugly, deceptive, competitors, threats, and not trustworthy. We see them this way because this is exactly who *we are* without God's forgiveness. We project how we feel about ourselves on others and the world around us. However, when we take on the mindset of our new life in Christ, the mindset of love, grace, and forgiveness, we see ourselves through the cross. We see ourselves through Jesus.

When we see ourselves the way that God sees us, and feel about ourselves the way the God feels about us with the holiest of love, we begin to see people through the cross. We begin to see people through God's eyes. We begin to see people through Jesus. This is what Paul means when he says, "May I never boast except in the cross of our Lord Jesus Christ, through which the world has been crucified to me, and I to the world." This is what it means to be holy. Rather than having a mind of hostility and resentment about people in the world because of our own shame, guilt, fear, and doubt, we have a mind of love, grace, forgiveness, peace and joy.

To have a renewed mind is to embrace the forgiveness of God through Jesus that drives the spirit of the old nature out of our minds. This is to be holy. This is the likeness of God.

> Those who live according to the sinful nature have their minds set on what that nature desires; but those who live in accordance with the Spirit have their minds set on what the Spirit desires. The mind of sinful man is death, but the mind controlled by the Spirit is life and peace. (Rom 8:5–8)

> [You were taught] to be made new in the attitude of your minds; and to put on the new self, created to be like God in true righteousness and holiness. (Eph 4:23)

DISCIPLINING THE MIND

The everyday challenge of Christ-followers is to focus their minds on Christ and his agenda for the day. "Set your minds on things above, not on earthly things" (Col 3:2; cf. Phil 3:19; 4:8). To "fix" means to "mend" as in fixing a leaky faucet, to "fasten," as to attach a bracket to a wall, and to "rig" or "tamper" with as in fixing the outcome of a game. The believer *mends* his wayward attention and inbred distractions, *fastens* his attention on unseen reality, and *rigs* the outcome to more and more see heaven in places and situations where he saw only shadows before. In Greek, to "fix" means simply "an intensity of gaze," a determined, attentive searching out.

A frequently heard comment today is, "Keep an open mind." It generally means to wait until you know all the facts before firming up an opinion or conclusion. Not a bad idea! It can, however, be a very ambiguous term taken to mean an objective, unbiased approach to ideas but is a call for perpetual skepticism, for holding no firm convictions and granting plausibility to anything.

A *closed mind*, on the other hand, is usually taken to mean an attitude that is impervious to ideas, arguments, facts, and logic. "Don't confuse me with the facts; my mind is made up."

Christ-followers need an *open mind* to truth from whatever source, measuring all knowledge by the Word of God. An *open mind* to the Spirit allows for new insights into God's truth and revelation. Believers need an active mind that is willing to examine ideas critically to discern good from evil, falsehood from truth, to reach firm convictions and hold to them, to exercise creativity.

James 3:13–18 deserves careful scrutiny. James makes it clear that there are two kinds of wisdom: (1) earthly, and (2) heavenly. Earthly wisdom, he says, fosters bitter envy, selfish ambition, disorder, and every evil practice. On the other hand, spiritual wisdom that comes down from heaven demonstrates itself in proper living and by deeds done in humility. It is "first of all pure; then peace-loving, considerate, submissive, full of mercy and good fruit, impartial and sincere" (James 3:17, NIV). True wisdom rests in knowing the difference.

John warns us to not believe every spirit but to test them (1 John 4:1–3). Many false prophets have gone out into the world. What was true in John's day is no less true today. Discernment is needed even when watching so-called Christian television. Paul warns the Ephesians of every wind of teaching and the cunning and craftiness of men in their deceitful scheming (4:14). False teachers still abound while babes in Christ are often misled, spiritually gullible. A mind fixed on Christ is essential for proper learning.

Believers also need *closed minds,* closed to worldly wisdom and filthy content.

In an age when pornography is so easily accessible, followers of Christ must make a covenant with their minds to keep the meditations of their hearts pure and acceptable to God.

Dr. E. Stanley Jones, beloved missionary to India, was an occasional speaker in our college chapel. One year he was our speaker at our (Charles) spiritual emphasis week. Every evening he began his message with the same statement, "Whatever gets your attention, gets you." Students may have forgotten much of what else he had to say but many had difficulty getting away from that opening statement. We daily have the choice of controlling our thoughts or being controlled by them.

> That time of business does not with me differ from the time of prayer; and in the noise and clatter of my kitchen while several persons are at the same time calling for different things, I possess God in as great tranquility as if I were upon knees at the blessed sacrament.[2]

Such were the words of Brother Lawrence. The developing of an attitude of dependence and a constant realization that one lives in the very

---

2. Brother Lawrence, *Practice of the Presence*, 6.

presence of God contributes greatly to keeping one's mind focused on him. An old gospel songs refrains,

> Wonderful, wonderful, Jesus. In my heart He implanteth a song. A song of deliverance of courage and strength, in my heart He implanteth a song.

The song is both a challenge and a reminder to hide God's Word in one's heart as well as biblically-based hymns and choruses that the Holy Spirit will bring to mind to help keep it focused on him. Songs, implanted in our minds, are a reminder to recognize God's presence in both the good times and the trying times. He is there to comfort us when we trust him.

THE MIND'S GREATEST CHALLENGE

> For my thoughts are not your thoughts, neither are your ways my ways, declares the Lord. (Isa 55:8)

There are perhaps no more beautiful and poetic words in Scripture than 1 Corinthians 2:9. Every believer should commit them to memory but don't do so without memorizing verse 10 as well. Its message makes all the difference.

> No eye has seen, no ear has heard, no mind has conceived what God has prepared for those who love him—but God has revealed it to us by his Spirit. (1 Cor 2:9 NIV)

Paul makes it clear that we can know God's thoughts and discern his ways for we have the mind of Christ (v. 16).

David's charge to Solomon is a charge to every Spirit-filled believer:

> And you, my son Solomon, acknowledge the God of your father, and serve him with wholehearted devotion and with a willing mind, for the Lord searches every heart and understands every motive behind the thoughts . . . The Lord has chosen you to build a temple as a sanctuary. Be strong and do the work. (1 Chron. 28:9–10, NIV)

SOME QUESTIONS TO CONSIDER

1. Are you capable each day to suggest to the Lord that he make your thoughts your prayers?

2. Have you ever memorized a verse of Scripture to quote when tempted to think thoughts that would be displeasing to the Lord? What is it?

3. On what do you focus when you have nothing else to think about?

A HYMN FOR MEDITATION: MAY THE MIND OF CHRIST, MY SAVIOR

May the mind of Christ, my Savior,
Live in me from day to day,
By His love and power controlling
All I do and say.

May the Word of God dwell richly
In my heart from hour to hour,
So that all may see I triumph
Only through His power.

May the peace of God my Father
Rule my life in everything, That I may be calm to comfort
Sick and sorrowing.

May the love of Jesus fill me
As the waters fill the sea;
Him exalting, self-abasing,
This is victory.

May I run the race before me,
Strong and brave to face the foe, Looking only unto Jesus
As I onward go.

May His beauty rest upon me,
As I seek the lost to win, And may they forget the channel,
Seeing only Him.

Relatively little is known of English hymn writer Kate Barclay Wilkinson, born in England in 1859. She was known to have ministered to young women in west London and to have been associated with the Keswick "deeper life" Convention. Only one of her hymns survives, the content of which is indeed rich. The hymn was written in the early twentieth century and is based on Paul's words in Philippians 2:5, "Have this mind among yourselves, which is yours in Christ Jesus."

What does Wilkinson mean when she connects the mind of Christ, the Word of God, the peace of God, and the love of Jesus? The mind of Christ can, indeed, control our lives in all we do and say as it is nurtured in the Word of God, which activity produces his peace reigning and ruling our lives, constraining us by his love that we might seek more of him and less of self. The mind of Christ changes our focus, *looking only unto Jesus, seeing only him*.

Jesus is the example of one who was willing to surrender his rights and to humbly take the place of a servant; the opposite of what humanity's sinful nature is prone to do. When our mind and will are surrendered to him, we give up our rights and choose the path of service to others.

7

BODY

Do you not know that your body is a temple of the Holy Spirit within you, whom
you have from God? You are not your own, for you were bought with a price. So
glorify God in your body. —1 Corinthians 6:19–20 (NIV)

One of the most awesome truths of the Bible is that the Holy Spirit
takes up his residence in our bodies when Christ comes into our lives.
Understanding the implications of that truth can be revolutionary. How
awesome to think of our body as the temple of the Holy Spirit.

In the Epistle to the Romans, Paul observes an interesting contrast.
In chapter one, speaking of fallen humanity, Paul says, they exchanged the
truth of God for a lie, and worshiped and served the creature rather than
the Creator (v. 25). Yet in chapter 9, he speaks of those who ask, "Why
did you make me like this?" To which, Paul questions, does not the potter
have the right to make out of the same lump of clay some pottery for noble
purposes and some for common use? (v. 21).

Still today, there are those who *worship* the body while others *despise*
theirs. Recently a TV commercial for a plastic surgeon has him exclaiming,
"I have spent my adult life making people's bodies beautiful." The amount
of money spent annually by Americans to change their physical appearance
is staggering. At the same time, people who are struggling with acceptance
of their bodies as God chose to create them spend millions on counselors.

Between the two extremes is a wholesome self-acceptance and real-ization of biblical truth about our bodies. God made us the way he did for a purpose and gives to each of us a tool to use in honoring him. Some choose to sell their bodies for monetary gain, others carelessly give little or no attention to how they use their bodies, while others purchase changes on their bodies seeking to improve their appearance. The way one views and uses his or her body speaks loudly of the inner condition of the heart.

A temple is a holy place and so is our body, for the Holy Spirit dwells therein. Therefore, we are not to sin against our bodies. The Bible says we are not to:

1. **Disfigure our bodies.** In Leviticus 19:28 the Israelites were told not to cut their bodies or put tattoos on themselves. Finding fault with the creature is finding fault with the Creator.

2. **Dress immodestly.** In 1 Timothy 2:9, Paul instructs women that they should dress modestly and with decency. The way both men and women dress should never be an enticement for someone to sin. In contrast Peter suggests that a woman's beauty be "the hidden person of the heart with the imperishable beauty of a gentle and quiet spirit, which in God's sight is very precious." (1 Pet 3:4)

3. **Destroy our bodies with drugs and/or alcohol.** "If anyone destroys God's temple, God will destroy him. For God's temple is holy, and you are that temple." (1 Cor 3:17)

4. **Degrade our bodies in sexual sin.** In 1 Corinthians 6:19 Paul commands believers to "flee sexual sin." Sexual activity between two persons outside of marriage is sin. Paul ends the chapter with a sober word of warning and a sensible word of challenge, "For you were bought with a price. So glorify God in your body." (1 Cor 6:20)

The Bible says we are to dedicate the parts of our bodies to righteous living. Romans 6:13 says, "Do not present your members to sin as instruments for unrighteousness, but present yourselves to God as those who have been brought from death to life, and your members to God as instruments for righteousness."

We can take our eyes for example. In Habakkuk 1:13 we are told that God's eyes "are too pure to look on evil" (NIV), and Job 31:1 tells us that Job had made "a covenant with his eyes not to look lustfully at a girl" (NIV). In the Sermon on the Mount, Jesus warned his audience, "If your right eye causes you to sin, gouge it out and throw it away . . . and if your right hand causes you to sin, do the same. It is better for you to lose one part of your body than for your whole body to go into hell" (Matt 5:28–30, NIV).

Dietrich Bonhoeffer wrote,

> Adherence to Jesus allows no free rein to desire unless it be accompanied by love. Instead of trusting to the unseen, we prefer the tangible fruits of desire. . .Lust is impure because it is unbelief, and therefore it is to be shunned. No sacrifice is too great if it enables us to conquer a lust which cuts us off from Jesus . . . When you have made your eye the instrument of impurity, you cannot see God with it.[1]

The simple act of daily yielding the members of one's body to the Lord serves as a strong antidote to many sins and heartaches otherwise experienced by man.

DELAY IMMEDIATE GRATIFICATION

Dedicating our bodies also includes a willingness to delay immediate gratification for the accomplishment of a more valuable objective.

"It's crazy to marry someone without living with them first. You need to test out the relationship before making a commitment!" Before you believe that statement, give it some serious thought. With an estimated 70 percent of US couples cohabiting before marriage and all of the conflicting reports of recent studies as to the rightness or wrongness of doing so, it would certainly be worthwhile to consider what God says about the subject.

Conflicting reports do abound. One social scientist conducts a study that encourages the practice while another quotes statistics to prove that couples whom first cohabit have a greater chance of later getting a divorce. Who are we to believe? Why not ask the One with whom the whole idea of marriage had it origin? "Let marriage be held in honor among all, and let the marriage bed be undefiled, for God will judge the sexually immoral and adulterous" (Heb 13:4). Need any more be said?

There is something very sacred about a wedding conducted in a church, but how can a couple who have cohabited stand before the altar of a church and ask God's blessing on their union if their relationship has been previously adulterous? Pastors are frequently placed in a precarious

---

1. Bonhoeffer, *Cost of Discipleship*, ch. 10.

situation when asked to marry couples whom are already living together. A pastor truly committed to the Word of God will not do so unless the couple is first willing to separate until the day of their ceremony while seeking God's forgiveness for their past sin.

"Slightly soiled but greatly reduced in price," read the sign in the window. The merchandise for sale was the remnant of a fire that had ravaged the local department store a few days earlier. The Spirit of God was using the message of the sign, however, to bring deep conviction to the young, single gal who was living life freely. She read the sign as she walked by the store on her lunch break.

She had been enjoying the pleasures of sin for a season, after which, she felt dirty and unfulfilled. Her feelings of self-worth were at an all-time low. Tremendous conflict existed in her thoughts. She was only doing what other friends were doing. They were taught that there were no moral absolutes. Convictions she had been taught were old-fashioned and people didn't think that way anymore. What might be wrong for someone else doesn't necessarily mean that it is wrong for you.

To compound the conviction of the sin, she had sat through a pastor's Sunday sermon that spoke of the body as a temple of the Holy Spirit. The Spirit's conviction was profound. No longer did the lure of her previous lifestyle look glamorous to her. But how could she ever change? Change would surely require the giving up of some of her closest friends. It might even mean spending lonely weekends without friends with whom to socialize. She might even be giving up the opportunity to find the man of her dreams.

She did remember the singles group back at the church she had attended on occasion, when it was convenient. She actually helped start the group but soon dropped out when the group began to espouse moral values with which she did not agree. Maybe they weren't so wrong after all. At least, they seemed to be a group of singles who enjoyed life and had a sense of purpose even though their thoughts about having fun didn't quite hook her attention.

The next weekend came. Her previous plans had fallen through. Why spend the evening alone? Why not go back and revisit the singles group that met in the church's recreational center? The warmth of the welcome she received was a bit overwhelming. They seemed to treat her as if she had never left. Soon she was enjoying meaningful dialogue with several very impressive singles, both male and female.

After attending their events for a couple of weeks, she found herself attending church more frequently. The pastor's sermons made more sense to her than they had before. Some Sundays she was sure he was speaking directly to her. At the end of the service, however, she felt dirty and longed to be clean. She responded to the Spirit, not in church, but at home by her bedside as she cried out to the Lord for a new beginning. God met her in her bedroom.

Although she felt it too private to speak freely of her past, she confessed to the group her desire to use her life, her body, mind and spirit to glorify the Lord and to please him in all she did. A trip to a mission field one summer began to change her total sense of direction in life. A young man on the trip wasn't all that bad either. He had similar desires and together they explored the option of serving the Lord together.

DEVELOP GOOD HABITS

"For no one ever hated his own flesh, but nourishes and cherishes it, just as Christ does the church" (Eph 5:29). Obesity has reached epidemic proportions in America. Many medical expenses are directly related to obesity; yet, Christians have often been judgmental of the alcoholic or drug addict while paying no attention to their own abuse of the body by overeating.

In 2014 Americans were reported by the America's Health Ranking to be fatter and more slothful than the previous year. The obesity rate was reported at 29.4%, with nearly a quarter of people reporting no physical activity or exercise in the last thirty days, thereby doubling in the past twenty-five years. Obesity is a leading contributor to death in the United States and is tied to chronic, costly diseases, which are bedeviling the healthcare system.

The term "couch potato" was coined in the 1970s to denote a sedentary lifestyle as a type of lifestyle with very little, or irregular physical activity. Sedentary activities include sitting, reading, watching television, playing video games and using the computer for much of the day with little or no vigorous physical exercise. A sedentary lifestyle can contribute to many preventable causes of death. An excessive amount of time a person spends watching a screen such as a television, computer monitor, or a mobile device is linked to negative health consequences. Regular exercise can easily be described as a holy habit.

In 1 Timothy 4:7b–8 Paul uses the language of the athlete: "Train [exercise, KJV] yourself to be godly. For physical exercise is of some value, but godliness has value for all things, holding promise for both the present life and the life to come" (NIV).

Train, exercise, discipline all can be used to translate Paul's intention; the word in the original language is the word from which we get gymnasium. Although, by comparison physical exercise compared to spiritual discipline fades in value, Paul still identifies it as valuable, and *Wikipedia* agrees:

> Physical exercise is any bodily activity that enhances or maintains physical fitness and overall health and wellness. It is performed for various reasons, including strengthening muscles and the cardiovascular system, honing athletic skills, weight loss or maintenance, and merely enjoyment. Frequent and regular physical exercise boosts the immune system and helps prevent the "diseases of affluence" such as heart disease, cardiovascular disease, Type 2 diabetes, and obesity. It may also help prevent depression, help to promote or maintain positive self-esteem, and improve mental health generally. Health care providers often call exercise the "miracle" or "wonder" drug—alluding to the wide variety of proven benefits that it can provide.[2]

Sounds pretty convincing. Physical exercise requires discipline and we live amidst an undisciplined society. One only has to look around to see strong evidences of that fact both in society and the church.

Discipline is the "D" word! Not the most desirable word in our vocabulary but one that pays tremendous dividends. The value and absolute necessity of discipline, when joined with a correlating virtue of accountability can actually lengthen the years of a believer's life. Discipline and accountability go hand-in-hand.

Spiritual maturity and physical fitness will only come when we put that principle to practice. Will to be disciplined and welcome accountability.

Discipline means regularity, routine, commitment. It means living intentionally. It means saying "no" to some things that are good but not best for us. It's saying "yes" even when we don't feel like it, because we know it's good for us. Discipline is an act of our wills. It is not easy, even harder for some than others. Yet, discipline pays huge dividends.

2. *Wikipedia*, s.v. "Physical Exercise."

Accountability requires two. No lone rangers. Accountability is a motivator to want to do the right things and see the right results. We want to look good in the eyes of the other. It's embarrassing not to have tried, to compromise our priorities, to have shown weakness in the presence of temptation. Accountability binds us in a relationship that goes beyond the surface and leads us to a caring relationship with another. An accountability partner is a valuable possession.

Whether growing spiritually or physically, discipline and accountability are paramount. Continue to ponder those words and the value they have for your life and especially for your relationship with him, whom though you cannot see, you love and want to please.

DEAL WITH ADDICTIVE BEHAVIORS

Ephesians 4:19 addresses the progression of addiction in behavior: temptation > experimentation > addiction > escalation > de-sensitivity > acting out. Paul, on the other hand, advises that no one need be bound by sinful behavior. "Everything is permissible for me but I will not be mastered by anything" (1 Cor 6:12 NIV). Earlier in the chapter (vv. 9–11), he addresses those who once were bound by sexual immorality, idolatry, thievery, materialism, drinking, slandering and swindling. "And this is what some of you were. But you were washed, you were sanctified, you were justified in the name of the Lord Jesus Christ and by the Spirit of our God." No one need be bound and those who are can be set free.

The success of Alcoholics Anonymous (AA) is well established in our country. AA has helped more men and women out of their personal bondage than perhaps any other organization or program. One must not forget, however, that their initial appeal is to a greater power. As believers in Christ, we know his name and have even a greater resource than the AA Manual. The Word of God is not silent on the matter of freedom from bondage.

Those who have addictive behaviors would do well to begin by asking a soul-searching question proposed by Paul,

> When you were slaves to sin, you were free from the control of righteousness. What benefit did you reap at that time from the things you are now ashamed of? Those things result in death. But now that you have been set free from sin and have become slaves

to God, the benefit you reap leads to holiness, and the result is eternal life. (Rom 6:20–22, NIV)

One would benefit by re-reading the question, exchanging his addictive behavior for the words "sins and the things." The question is most relevant and penetrating. Next, the submitting of oneself to divine therapy puts one on the road to freedom (Rom 12:1–2) suggests a dual response. Offer your body. Renew your mind.

Begin with a new way of thinking. There is one thing we know for sure. The Holy Spirit indwells our body. Our body belongs to Christ and when Christ died, we died with him. Faith in Christ's death breaks the power of sin in our lives. We do not have to live in bondage. Pornography, alcohol, and drugs partially satisfy the desires of the flesh. The Holy Spirit frees us to satisfy those same desires in an honorable way (Eph. 4:22–23).

We can exchange a corrupted attitude for a holy one, pursuing personal holiness. We can discipline our thoughts and fantasies to focus on that which is pure, bringing every thought into captivity to the Spirit (Matt 5:27–28; Job 31:1; Phil 4:8).

We can adopt a new way of behaving. Honoring God with our bodies is the daily challenge of every believer. We are to live so that as others look at us, they will see the reflection of Christ. Living a holy life is following the counsel of Paul in Romans chapter 6, "knowing our old self was crucified with Christ" (v. 6), we "reckon" our self "dead to sin but alive to God" (v. 11), and "yield the parts of our body to him as instruments of righteousness" (v. 13).

When tempted to sin, we claim the promise of God in 1 Corinthians 10:13 that "with every temptation there comes a way of escape." When our will is surrendered to his will, we will to do his will and claim victory over the temptation.

It is God's will that you should be sanctified: that you should avoid sexual immorality; that each of you should learn to control his own boy in a way that is holy and honorable, not in passionate lust like the heathen, who do not know God (1 Thess 4:3–4).

We can live a holy life.

SOME QUESTIONS TO CONSIDER

1. However you have used your body in the past cannot be undone but can be forgiven and forgotten of God. Is there room for repentance to be sure the blood of Christ covers the past?

2. Is there any area of bondage in your life? Do you truly believe that God can give you freedom over it?

3. What, if anything, must change in your life in order to make your body an even greater tool to glorify your Lord? Do you regularly yield the members of your body as servants of righteousness?

4. What role does discipline play in your life?

A HYMN FOR MEDITATION: TAKE MY LIFE AND LET IT BE

"I went for a little visit of five days," wrote Frances Havergal, explaining what prompted her to write her well-known hymn, "Take My Life and Let It Be."

> There were ten persons in the house; some were unconverted and long prayed for, some converted but not rejoicing Christians. God gave me the prayer, "Lord, give me all in this house." And He just did. Before I left the house, everyone had got a blessing. The last night of my visit I was too happy to sleep and passed most of the night in renewal of my consecration, and those little couplets formed themselves and chimed in my heart one after another till they finished with "ever only, ALL FOR THEE!"[3]

It was on this day, February 4, 1874, that Frances wrote the hymn that is still sung around the world.

One of the most dedicated Christian women of the nineteenth century, Frances was the youngest child of a Church of England minister. Though she was always in frail health, she led an active life, encouraging many people to turn to Jesus and others to seek a deeper spiritual walk. Frances had begun reading and memorizing the Bible at the age of four, eventually memorizing the Psalms, Isaiah, and most of the New Testament.

3. "Frances Havergal Wrote 'Take My Life and Let it Be,'" Church History Timeline, 1801–1900, Christianity.com.

At seven she wrote her first poems. Several of her mature verses became hymns. In addition to "Take My Life," she wrote such favorites as "I Gave My Life for Thee," "Like a River Glorious," and "Who Is on the Lord's Side?"

Frances was often in demand as a concert soloist. She also was a brilliant pianist and learned several modern languages as well as Greek and Hebrew. With all her education, however, Frances Havergal maintained a simple faith and confidence in her Lord. She never wrote a line of poetry without praying over it. One of the lines of Frances Havergal's hymn says, "Take my silver and my gold; not a mite would I withhold." In 1878, four years after writing the hymn, Miss Havergal wrote a friend, "The Lord has shown me another little step, and, of course, I have taken it with extreme delight. 'Take my silver and my gold' now means shipping off all my ornaments to the Church Missionary House, including a jewel cabinet that is really fit for a countess, where all will be accepted and disposed of for me . . . nearly fifty articles are being packed up. I don't think I ever packed a box with such pleasure."[4]

TAKE MY LIFE AND LET IT BE

Take my life and let it be, Consecrated, Lord, to Thee. Take my moments and my days, Let them flow in endless praise.

Take my hands and let them move, At the impulse of Thy love. Take my feet and let them be, Swift and beautiful for Thee.

Take my voice and let me sing, Always, only for my King. Take my lips and let them be, Filled with messages from Thee.

Take my silver and my gold, Not a mite would I withhold. Take my intellect and use, Every power as Thou shalt choose.

Take my will and make it Thine, It shall be no longer mine. Take my heart, it is Thine own, It shall be Thy royal throne.

Take my love, my Lord, I pour, At Thy feet its treasure store. Take myself and I will be, Ever, only, all for Thee.

4. Ibid.

8

LOVE

You shall love the Lord your God with all your heart and with all your soul and
with all your mind. This is the great and first commandment. And a second is
like it: You shall love your neighbor as yourself. On these two commandments
depend all the Law and the Prophets. —Matthew 22:37–40

Faith is the mother of us all; with Hope following in her train and Love of God
and Christ and neighbor leading the way. Let a man's mind be wholly bent on
these, and he has fulfilled all the demands of holiness; for to possess Love is to be
beyond the reach of sin. — The Epistle of Polycarp to the Philippians

If there is any word, four letters or not, that best sums up a holy life, it is
love. From the lips of the apostle, "Now these three remain: faith hope
and love. But the greatest of these is love" (1 Cor 13:13 NIV). From the lips
of our Lord, in response to an expert in the law, the greatest commandment
is to "love the Lord you God with all your heart, soul and mind . . . the first
and greatest commandment and the second is like it: Love your neighbor
as yourself" (Matt 22:37–40). However, individuals in and of themselves
incapable of that kind of love. Where can such love be found?

THE SOURCE OF LOVE

"We love because he first loved us" (1 John 4:19, NIV). F. F. Bruce, in his commentary *The Epistles of John,* writes, "God's love for us, then supplies the motive power for His people's love for one another . . . they must be loving because He is loving—not with the 'must' of external compulsion but with the 'must' of inward constraint; God's love is poured into their hearts by the Holy Spirit whom they have received."[1] God is love (Gk. *agape*), therefore, God is love's source. He alone can provide the incentive and power to love as he loves. The love of Christ indeed constrains and enables us to love.

The word *agape* was used by the early Christians to refer to the self-sacrificing love of God for humanity. When 1 John 4:8 says, "God is love," the Greek New Testament uses the word *agape* . C. S. Lewis, in his book *The Four Loves,* used *agape* to describe what he believed was the highest level of love known to humanity—a selfless love, a love that was passionately committed to the well-being of the other.

Anglican theologian O. C. Quick (1885–1944) suggests that

> if we could imagine the love of one who loves men purely for their own sake, and not because of any need or desire of his own, purely desires their good, and yet loves them wholly, not for what at this moment they are, but for what he knows he can make of them because he made them, then we should have in our minds some true image of the love of the Father and Creator of mankind.[2]

One of the most creative expressions of the love of God can be found in the familiar hymn *The Love of God.* The story of the hymn is somewhat conjecture. Some believe that similar wording of the third verse can be found as early as the *Qu'ran*:

> If all the trees on earth were pens, and the ocean were ink, replenished by seven more oceans, the writing of God's wonderful signs and creations would not be exhausted; surely God is All-Mighty, All-Wise.[3]

The author of the hymn, Frederick Lehman, asserts that the third stanza, "Could we with ink the ocean fill," had been found penciled on the

---

1. Bruce, *Epistles of John,* 109.

2. Quick, *Doctrines of the Creed,* 55.

3. Ayat Luqman 31:27.

wall of a patient's room in an insane asylum after he had been carried to his grave.

It is further conjecture that the patient had adapted the words from a Jewish author's poem, the roots of which go back to the eleventh century and is attributed to a Rabbi Joseph Marcus. The poem is known as the "Haddamut," written at the beginning of the eleventh century. Whatever the origin of the third verse, it is interesting to know that Christians and Jews share the sentiments of the song of praise to God for his love.

As early as Genesis 24:63 we hear of Isaac, a godly man, investing time in meditation. Try meditating on the words of the hymn.

> The love of God is greater far, Than tongue or pen can ever tell; It goes beyond the highest star, And reaches to the lowest hell; The guilty pair, bowed down with care, God gave His Son to win; His erring child He reconciled, And pardoned from his sin. Could we with ink the ocean fill, And were the skies of parchment made, Were every stalk on earth a quill, And every man a scribe by trade; To write the love of God above Would drain the ocean dry; Nor could the scroll contain the whole, Though stretched from sky to sky. Oh, love of God, how rich and pure! How measureless and strong! It shall forevermore endure—The saints' and angels' song.

THE COMMAND TO LOVE

> Be imitators of God, therefore, as dearly loved children and live a life of love, just as Christ loved us and gave himself up for us as a fragrant offering and sacrifice to God. (Eph 5:2, NIV)

THE POWER OF LOVE

Thomas Chalmers (1780–1847) was one of the most prolific pastors and teachers that Scotland and the world ever knew. *The Expulsive Power of a New Affection* is perhaps his most famous work. It is one of the most popular sermons young seminarians ever study.

Addressing the biblical admonition, "Love not the world, neither the things that are in the world. If any man loves the world, the love of the Father is not in him" (1 John 2:15 KJV), Chalmers communicated his objective at the beginning of the message. His purpose was to show that the love of world could best be replaced by exchanging it for a new affection rather than attempting to withdraw one's regard from an object that is deemed unworthy of it. Three of the main points of the sermon include:

1. Misplaced affections need to be replaced by the far greater power of the affection of the Gospel.

2. A new affection is more successful in replacing an old affection than simply trying to end it without supplanting it with something better.

3. It is not enough to understand the worthlessness of the world; one must value the worth of the things of God.

With joy believers sing, "Turn your eyes upon Jesus, look full in his wonderful face and the things of earth will grow strangely dim in the light of his glory and grace." It is a joy to sing and yet a far greater joy to experience. When the believer lives a holy lifestyle, he soon discovers the dimness of the world and the brightness of his glory and grace. When bad habits are broken, success continues when the void is filled with grace.

THE PERFECTING OF LOVE

The Message paraphrases 1 John 4:17–18 this way: "Well informed love banishes fear. Since fear is crippling, a fearful life—fear of death, fear of judgment—is one not yet fully formed in love." The NIV adds a practical application, "God is love." Whoever lives in love lives in God and God in him. In this way, love is made complete among us so that we will have confidence on the day of judgment because in this world we are like him. These verses make it obvious that we grow in love, and we grow in love by loving. Purity is not maturity.

HOW DO YOU RIPEN THE FRUIT OF LOVE?

First, begin by measuring your love. Evaluate yourself according to the characteristics of love as found in 1 Corinthians 13. Do so by substituting your name for the word "love" each time that it appears.

The Characteristics of Agape Love: 1 Corinthians 13:4–7

1. **Love is patient** (v. 4). Far from anger or wrath, long-suffering, not re-taliating, makes allowance for others faults, calms quarrels, promotes unity; waits patiently on others and circumstances rather than getting angry and acting prematurely without due regard for the interests of others. "When they hurled their insults at him he did not retaliate; when he suffered, he made no threats" (1 Pet 2:23 NIV).

2. **Love is kind** (v. 4). Kindness shows undeserved generosity, bestowing benefits, cares more for others than for one's self, tender and compassionate, seeks the good of those who may be irritants to us. "See that no one repays anyone evil for evil, but always seek to do good to one another and to everyone" (1 Thess 5:15).

3. **Love does not envy** (v. 4). The absence of envy is contentment. Contentment does not compare oneself with others, does not want what others have, and rejoices in the successes of others, not offended when others are preferred before them. "I have learned the secret of being content in any and every situation" (Phil 4:12, NIV).

4. **Love does not boast, is not proud** (v. 4). Humility does not play the braggart, does not strut or have a swelled head, does not serve for the praise of man, lives for the glory of God. "Do not think of yourself more highly than you ought, but rather think of yourself with sober judgment, in accordance with the measure of faith God has given you" (Rom 12:3, NIV).

5. **Love is not rude** (v. 5). Courteousness goes beyond the rules of politeness, does not force oneself on others, observes decorum and good manners, does not act ill-mannered or display improper conduct.

6. **Love is not self-seeking** (v. 5). Unselfish—identifying with the other person, making his interests my own instead of insisting on my own way, crucified with Christ, concerned about the spiritual welfare of others, always seeking the will of God for each situation. "Father, if you are willing, take this cup from me; yet not my will, but yours be done" (Luke 22:42, NIV).

7. **Love is not angered** (v. 5). Even-tempered love does not yield to provocation, not embittered by injuries, does not fly off the handle. "But

now you must rid yourselves of all such things as these: anger, rage, malice, slander and filthy language from your lips" (Col 3:8, NIV).

8. **Love keeps no record of wrongs** (v. 5). Forgiveness does not take into account the sins of others, committed to abstain from slander, gossip, and harshness. Willing to forgive wrongs by not keeping an account of each harm with a view to future retaliation. "See to it that no one fails to obtain the grace of God; that no root of bitterness springs up and causes trouble, and by it many become defiled" (Heb 12:15).

9. **Love does not delight in evil** (v. 6). Righteousness does not revel when others stumble, is not glad when others go wrong. "Then neither do I condemn you . . . Go now and leave your life of sin" (John 8:11 ,NIV).

10. **Love rejoices with the truth** (v. 6). Love is truthful and thereby rejoices in the sound of and extension of what is true, does not compromise the truth for personal gain, is glad when the truth of a matter prevails. "The Lord detests lying lips, but he delights in men who are truthful" (Prov 12:22 NIV).

11. **Love always protects** (v. 7). Protective—to protect by covering, keeps confidential that which should be kept secret, does not pass on anything about anyone that would ultimately hurt them. "Do not let any unwholesome talk come out of your mouths, but only what is helpful for building others up according to their needs, that it may benefit those who listen" (Eph 4:29, NIV).

12. **Love always trusts** (v. 7). Love always thinks the best of others until given reason to believe otherwise, seeks to give the most favorable interpretation the truth will allow, believing the best, is not unduly suspicious, never gives up on people, does not gullibly accept unsubstantial rumors or reports about anyone. "Be completely humble and gentle; be patient, bearing with one another in love" (Eph. 4:2, NIV).

13. **Love always hopes** (v. 7). Love is optimistic. It wishes the best for others against all odds, redemption for the fallen, provision for the needy, takes the optimistic route, refuses to accept defeat, looks on the bright side of every situation. "We who are strong ought to bear with the failings of the weak and not to please ourselves. Each of us should please his neighbor for his good to build him up" (Rom 15:1–2, NIV).

14. **Love always perseveres** (v. 7). Love is persistent. It never looks back, bears adversity with a confident spirit, never gives up on people who are needy, exercises positive fortitude. "Blessed is the man who perseveres under trial because when he has stood the test, he will receive the crown of life that God has promised to those who love him" (Jas 1:12, NIV).

THE MODEL OF LOVE

Focus on love's perfect model. In the Sermon on the Mount Jesus set the standard for love. "Be perfect, therefore, as your heavenly Father is perfect" (Matt 5:48, NIV). Christ made a distinction between the ordinary standards of morality observed in the world and the standard at which his disciples should aim. Christian perfection is demonstrated when we learn to:

- forgive as God forgives
- love our enemies
- bless those who curse us
- pray for those who persecute us
- do good to those who hate us
- turn the other cheek
- give our cloak as well as our tunic
- go the extra mile
- give to those in need.

Over the years, numerous believers were enriched by the ministry and teaching of Chuck Colson. Since his death, Eric Metaxas, one of Colson's successors, has provoked many of us to think deeply about the real essence of Christian living. His *BreakPoint* presentations have challenged many.

Back in 2010, Eric reported on a story of murder and forgiveness. The story was about a couple named Andy and Kate Grosmaire. "The Grosmaires," Eric wrote, "received the kind of news that is every parent's worst nightmare: Their daughter, Ann, had been shot in the head by her fiancée, Conor McBride." Upon arriving at the hospital, Andy Grosmaire realized that apart from a miracle, his daughter, Ann would die. Ultimately she died. While standing by her bedside praying, her Dad felt he heard her say, "Forgive him." Feeling the pain of her death he felt he could not even consider such a request. However, he could not get away from repeatedly hearing her plea, "Forgive him."

When Conor McBride made out his visitation list, while serving his time in jail awaiting trial, he listed Andy's wife Kate as one of the people welcomed to visit him in jail. When she visited him she delivered a message to him from her husband, "Tell him I love him, and I forgive him."

The Grosmaires were demonstrating the very nature of Calvary love. Their love was not just in words but also in actions. They met the prosecutor who was to prosecute McBride. They were told that they had it in their power to affect the outcome of the trial. After meeting with Conor, they asked that he receive a ten-to fifteen-year sentence.

The prosecutor considered the family's wishes, but because he was representing the state's interest, insisted that McBride serve twenty years. Under Florida law he could have served a life sentence and may have been sentenced to death. The Grosmaires exercised their faith and the wisdom of warding off bitterness and anger by demonstrating the same kind of love demonstrated by Christ on the cross.

"The kind of forgiveness on display in this story is the antithesis of what Dietrich Bonhoeffer called cheap grace," wrote Eric Metaxas. "The Grosmaires are all too aware of the damage McBride caused, and they still feel the pain that that damage inflicted. As Kate Grosmaire told the *New York Times*, 'forgiving Conor doesn't change the fact that Ann is not with us . . . I walk by her empty bedroom at least twice a day.'"[4]

Later, Kate Grosmaire was reported as saying, "Conor owed us a debt he could never repay. And releasing him from that debt would release us from expecting that anything in this world could satisfy us."

Eric concluded his comments by saying,

> This kind of forgiveness is Christianity's greatest calling card. To be able to love those who have done you unimaginable harm and seek their good is truly wondrous. Other faiths speak about mercy and compassion. Some even urge you to "let go" of old wounds for your own sake. But Christians worship a savior who, even as he was unjustly executed, prayed for those who placed him on the cross and insists that those who profess his name love their enemies, not just their friends.[5]

4. Metaxes, "Murder, Justice . . . and Forgiveness."

5. Ibid.

The standard is high, in fact, impossible, humanly speaking. Only through the enabling of the Holy Spirit that indwells the believer can he love as Jesus loves. When people live not for themselves but for others, the love of Christ is manifested through them. The holy life is the life of the love of God manifest in and through us by the forgiveness of sin.

SOME QUESTIONS TO CONSIDER

1. Has God ever called on you to love someone who has seriously hurt you? How successful were you in doing so?

2. Have you ever experienced the enabling power of the Spirit, enabling you to do something you know you are, in and of yourself, incapable of doing?

3. Do you notice the down and out, the downtrodden the homeless and helpless?

4. Is love the language spoken in your home? If so, in what ways?

A HYMN FOR MEDITATION: LOVE DIVINE, ALL LOVES EXCELLING

Love divine, all loves excelling, Joy of heaven, to earth come down, Fix in us thy humble dwelling, All thy faithful mercies crown. Jesus, thou art all compassion, Pure unbounded love thou art Visit us with thy salvation, Enter every trembling heart.

Breathe, O breathe Thy loving Spirit, Into every troubled breast; Let us all in Thee inherit, Let us find that second rest. Take away the power of sinning; Alpha and Omega be; End of faith, as its beginning, Set our hearts at liberty.

Come, almighty to deliver, Let us all thy life receive; Suddenly return and never, Never more thy temples leave. Thee we would be always blessing, Serve Thee as thy hosts above, Pray, and praise thee, without ceasing, Glory in thy perfect love.

Finish then thy new creation, Pure and sinless let us be; Let us see thy great salvation, Perfectly restored in thee: Changed from glory into glory, Till in heaven we take our place, Till we cast our crowns before thee, Lost in wonder, love and praise.

This hymn was written by Charles Wesley with a theme of Christian perfection at its center. It is among Wesley's finest and better known hymns. It is found almost universally in general collections of the past century, including not only Methodist and Anglican hymn books, but also hymnals associated with Reformed, Presbyterian, Baptist, Lutheran, Pentecostal and Roman Catholic traditions, to name a few.

Specifically, it appears in 1,328 of the North American hymnals indexed by the online *Dictionary of North American Hymnology*, comparable to Newton's "Amazing Grace" (1,036), Wesley's "O for a Thousand Tongues" (1,249), and Watts' "When I Survey the Wondrous Cross" (1,483), though still well short of Toplady's "Rock of Ages" (2,139) or Wesley's own "Jesus, Lover of my Soul" (2,164).

THEOLOGICALLY-MOTIVATED ALTERATIONS

Over the years few hymns have been altered more as they were included in different hymnals. It is difficult to acquire a copy of the words as they were written originally. The passages which are most subject to change tend for the most part to be those that advance a distinctively Wesleyan "perfectionist" account of the Christian life (i.e., those that suggest that one can be completely cleansed of sin in this life, by means of a "second blessing" whereby committed and sanctified Christians rest wholly in God and may be said to share the holiness of Christ himself). Many—certainly including those of a more Calvinist persuasion—found this idea troublesome.

The second stanza, when it was not omitted altogether, offered, and continues to offer, two stumbling blocks for some theologically sensitive Christians. Line 4 asks, "Let us find that second rest"; and line 5, "Take away our power of sinning." The phrase "second rest," would seem an explicit reference to Wesleyan "second blessing" theology; and the request to be stripped even of the ability to sin doubtless seemed to many unrealistic at best and blasphemous or immoral at worst, as appearing to "be a prayer to take away our free moral agency."

The line, "Take away our power of sinning," is believed by some to be too strong. Would it not be better to soften it by saying, "Take away the love of sinning or the bent of the mind toward sin?" "Can God take away from us our power of sinning without taking away our power of free obedience?" some would ask.

"Second Rest" is very generally replaced, usually by thy "prom-ised" rest; or, later, by "the promised rest"; and, "the power of sinning by the love of sinning," or "our bent of (or 'to') sinning" (originally and still chiefly in Methodist collections).

The line "Let us all thy life receive," in stanza 3 was read as suspiciously perfectionist, hence the common alteration to "Let us all thy grace receive." The same is probably true of other oft-changed lines. "Finish then thy New Creation," in stanza 4 was often replaced by, "Carry on thy new creation," the latter suggesting an ongoing process of sanctification rather than its achievement; and "Let us see thy great salvation perfectly restored in Thee," frequently changed to ". . .our whole salvation/secured by Thee." Both of these changes were introduced by Augustus Toplady's collection of 1776.

"Pure and sinless let us be," in stanza 4 was toned down, or at least made less absolute, by alteration to, "Pure and holy," and similar substi-tutes, especially the very common, "Pure, unspotted and Pure and spotless." Several of the re-phrasings of "Love Divine," continue in circulation today.

So, what can be said of the debate? Can John or Charles Wesley ever justly be accused of espousing a relationship with God in which humanity is incapable of sinning, let alone, forfeit his free moral agency? Such is a false accusation and indicates a lack of understanding Wesley's theology.

The hymn can legitimately be labeled a prayer. Wesley prayed that God would "finish His new creation, pure and sinless let us be." He is not affirming something already accomplished but something in progress. Can something be pure without being sinless? Can man never stand before God completely cleansed from all sin? "And the blood of Jesus Christ his Son cleanses us from all sin" (1 John 1:7).

Of the words, "our power of, love of or bent toward sinning," the later seems to say it best and yet, don't they all say the same thing? There is within every person an inherited "bent toward sinning" which when cleansed by the Holy Spirit can cease to exist. People can know a bent toward not sin-ning. Otherwise the provision of Christ's atonement would seem anemic.

It's fascinating to read, even in *Wikipedia*, comments regarding Au-gustus Toplady's final words to the first stanza of the familiar "Rock of Ages" written in 1763.

> There has been speculation that, though Toplady was a Calvinist, the words, "Be of sin the double cure, Save from wrath, and make me pure," suggest that he agreed with the teachings of the Method-ist preacher under whom he received his religious conversion, and

of his contemporary, John Wesley, who taught the "double cure," in which a sinner is saved by the atonement of Jesus and cleansed from inbred sin by the infilling of the Holy Spirit.[6]

The debate strengthens the affirmation made in the introduction of this book. Christians often sing a greater theology than they truly believe and live.

6. *Wikipedia*, s.v. "Augustus Toplady."

9

REST

Come unto me, all you who are weary and burdened, and I will give you rest.
Take my yoke upon you and learn from me for I am gentle and humble in heart,
and you will find rest for your souls. For my yoke is easy and my burden is light.
—Matthew 11:28–30, NIV

Every notable philosophy, system of ethics, and religion of human history has
striven for the realization of this goal, rest, through harmonious peace. But no
one has ever attained to the realization of the universal self, which harmoniously
relates man to himself, to society, and to God and His limitless universe, except
through personal faith and commitment to Jesus Christ. —Gareth Cockerill,
Hebrews: A Commentary

It seems counter-intuitive to think of the holy life as one of rest. Most
often we associate spiritual disciplines and long-suffering with the way
of the holy life, and indeed, a holy lifestyle demands them. John Wesley
once wrote,

> Vain hope! That a child of Adam should ever expect to see the
> kingdom of Christ and God without striving, without "agonizing"
> first "to enter in at the strait gate"! That the one who was "conceived
> and born in sin," and whose "inward parts are very wickedness,"

should once entertain the thought of being "purified as his Lord is pure" unless he "tread in his steps," and "take up his cross daily."[1]

What strong words! How can we begin to reconcile these two realities? On the one hand, the way of holy living is one of bearing a cross daily, commitment to spiritual disciplines, and persecution. On the other hand, *rest* is at the center of a holy life. These two truths seem to contradict one another almost like centripetal and centrifugal forces working against one another. In this chapter we will deal with this paradox. Most particularly, we will treat the role and function of the Holy Spirit in God's great plan for salvation as the means for the manifestation of rest in the midst of a holy life.

JESUS, HEALING, AND REST

One of the most magnificent promises of Christ is his promise of *rest* as mentioned in the passage above from Matthew. The concept of rest appears frequently in the Bible, both in the Old Testament and the New. God's promise to Moses can be viewed as a *prototype* of Christ's promise to those who followed him.

In Exodus 33:14, God not only promised his presence to go through the wilderness with Moses and the Israelites but he also promised the Israelites rest from their slavery. For ten generations the Israelites suffered at the hand of their Egyptian task masters. They started working at a very young age and could continue on until physical strength gave out. Their livelihood and wellbeing meant unending work. This is a symbol of the human condition.

One of the first things that God does when delivering Israel from their slavery, is reorient their calendar around a day of rest. God commands that Israel's central point of reference on the weekly schedule would be rest; the Sabbath. Not only this, but according to the Jewish calendar, the day begins with rest at sundown and ends with work at sunrise. Rest is the priority; rest comes first.

This new calendar was intended to instruct God's people that he was now their source of life, not their own efforts and striving. He wanted his people to understand that it is at his hand that they find life and wellbeing, not at the hand of their own striving, sweating, and backbreaking work, only

1. Outler, *John Wesley's Sermons*, 30.

to be tired and hungry again the next day. When we come to Christ, the first thing he does is reorient our lives to his cup that is eternally overflowing.

We read about this in John 4 where Jesus speaks to a woman at a well. They are both thirsty and Jesus asks the woman to give him a drink while she's fetching her own water. There are several things that are uncomfortable about this passage. First, this woman should not be out alone in the middle of the day. This was inappropriate in this time and culture. For her to be alone in this manner attests to the fact that there is some sort of strife between her and her fellow members of society. We learn later in the story that she has ongoing marital problems that has caused her to be marginalized in her community. Second, this woman was a Samaritan and Jesus a Jew. These two people are not to speak to one another if not only because they were male and female. For Jesus to extend a hand and speak to this woman was doubly *taboo*.

The point is brought to the front when the woman says, "How is it that you, a Jew ask for a drink from me, a woman of Samaria?" (John 4:9). Jesus gets right to his point in his response when he says, "If you knew the gift of God, and who it is that is saying to you, 'Give me a drink,' you would have asked him, and he would have given you living water" (John 4:10). Jesus goes on to say, "Everyone who drinks of this water will be thirsty again, but whoever drinks of the water that I will give him will never be thirsty again. The water that I will give him will become in him a spring of water welling up to eternal life" (John 4:14).

So, what do we learn from this? We learn that the inner thirst of the soul that we constantly strive to satisfy Jesus alone can satiate. Our brokenness, represented in the brokenness of the Samaritan woman, that causes us to endlessly work for the approval of others and good standing with society, can never be healed from our own efforts. We know in the depths of our hearts that we will always succumb to our humanness. Our healing is beyond our own power. It is not, however, beyond Jesus' power. Jesus is able to heal us so that we can cease striving. Jesus strives on our behalf and suffers in our place so that our work to be accepted "is finished."

THE YOKE

This rest, promised by God to every believer, is inseparably linked to Jesus' yoke. A yoke is a bar, or frame of wood, by which two draft animals (usually oxen) are joined at the neck for working together, as for pulling a load or a plow. This is a symbol of *mutual and reciprocal servitude.* In Christ we are yoked to him in order to serve him and accomplish his purposes on earth. To take his yoke is to surrender oneself in obedience to his will and way. *His yoke is not lighter because he demands less but because he bears more of the load with us.* Taking Jesus' yoke is the way to experience his rest.

I (Charles) grew up a very independent person. In fact, in my senior year of high school I won an award that produced a partial scholarship toward my first year in college. The award was for being the most *self-reliant* senior in my class.

My commitment as a Christ-follower came when I was fifteen. I loved the Word of God and quickly moved to commit much of it to memory. I chose Proverbs 3:5–6 as my life verses. In reality, I quickly learned to trust the Lord in most areas of my life, but had great difficulty not leaning on my own understanding and strength.

When problems arose, I always felt adequate to handle them. I would, as a final resort, ask for the Lord's help, but even then, I always suggested to the Lord how the problem should be handled. Of course, the Lord never chose to do it my way. God's wisdom and way was always far better. I always set myself up for a frustrating problem-solving endeavor.

The problem stages of my life would have always been much shorter had I asked for the Lord's help as a first resort and yielded the solution to him rather than trust in my own wisdom or lack thereof. The day came when I experienced a problem significant enough that I didn't have a clue how to resolve it. I was forced to turn to the Lord in desperation. God did such a work in my life that I was never again to use the Lord as a final resort.

The Lord showed me that my major problem was pride. My best response to problem solving was dependency. The Lord used two characters from the Old Testament to teach me a valuable lesson, Jehoshaphat and Hezekiah.

> Jehoshaphat also said to the king of Israel, "First seek the counsel of the Lord." (1 Kgs 22:5, NIV)

> Hezekiah received the letter from the messengers and read it. Then he went up to the temple of the Lord and spread it out before the Lord. (2 Kgs 19:14, NIV)

I learned that I could put the difficult situations of my life into God's hands and rest in him to bring about his perfect will and plan. No more striving in my own strength. Dependency replaced the feeling of sufficiency; rest replaced my struggle to trust in my own wisdom.

The first chapter of Colossians ends with Paul affirming, "Him we proclaim, warning everyone and teaching everyone with all wisdom, that we may present everyone mature in Christ. For this I toil, struggling with all his energy that he powerfully works within me" (Col 1:28–29).

A recent book title caught my attention, *The Utter Relief of Holiness*. In the book, well-known author, John Eldredge writes, "What a relief it would be to be set free from all that plagues us—the inner struggle with anger, or contempt, the habitual sins."[2] His book declares that the pursuit of a holy lifestyle provides that relief. Such a life is possible through Christ.

A return to the analogy of the yoke and reference to oxen can take us back to the difficulty Saul of Tarsus found in "kicking against the pricks." When our will is aligned with his and we are yoked together allowing him to lead; we find the *easiness* of his yoke—we find rest.

REST: A BROADER, BIBLICAL PERSPECTIVE

Furthermore, the biblical concept of rest is multi-dimensional. This is also true of our own modern understanding of rest. When we talk about "restlessness," for example, there is a sense of worry, or anxiety. I'm quite restless during takeoff and landing when flying. I (Matt) also get restless when it is time to preach. There's a sense of nervousness or anxiety inherent in the idea of "restlessness."

We can also talk about the need for proper physical rest. Our bodies need proper rest to regenerate. Our physical strength, like our spiritual strength, is limited. In this sense, the word "rest" implies the absence of effort, or ceasing to work. This also means that rest is productive.

I (Matt)used to be a server in a restaurant. In an average shift, I would walk about seven miles weaving in and out of tables, running back and forth from the kitchen, delivering drinks, appetizers, condiments, entrées and desserts. At the end of a shift, my back was sore and my dogs were barking! My body needed to cease working and rest.

Thinking about rest this way helps us to see that rest is actually productive! It is during times of rest that our bodies have a chance to refresh and restore. It is when we stop and relax that the body has the opportunity to do its work in restoring itself. This is one of the concepts at the heart of

2. Eldredge, *Utter Relief of Holiness* (from the book cover).

the Sabbath, which results as God's command for us to honor him with our rest.

These are just two modern notions of rest. But what of the biblical concept of rest as pertains to holy living and the saving love of Jesus? There are three types of rest that correspond to the holy life. The first is directly associated with the alleviation of the desperate and continuous worry that characterizes the human life when lived in separation from God. The psalmist describes this state in this way:

> My God, my God, why have your forsaken me? Why are you so far from saving me, from the worlds of my groaning? O my God, I cry by day, but you do not answer, and by night, *but I find no rest.* (Ps 22:1–2, emphasis added)

These precious words of David (that Jesus himself cites on the cross), once again, highlight the desperation of being separated from God.

The second is rest from striving in our own strength to please God or earn God's favor. When we receive the gift of faith something supernatural happens. *The Holy Spirit enters into our circumstances and makes his strength available to us.* Much in the same vein as the concept of physical rest described above, it is in our weakness that the power of the Holy Spirit is poured out upon us. It is in our weakness and our rest that we are made strong (Rom 8:26; 2 Cor 12:9; 13:4).

THE SABBATH: IT IS FINISHED

This concept links up once again with the concept of Sabbath. Why does God rest in the creation account? He obviously doesn't rest on the seventh day because he's tired from his creative activity. To the contrary, God's rest after the creation is a different kind of rest. God's resting after the six days of the creation is his way of stating that the job is *finished*—that all is done, and *complete*. There is nothing lacking in what he's created. This links up with Jesus' final words on the cross, "It is finished" (John 19:30). Jesus, like God the Father in the creation account, has completed his redemptive work through his suffering. With his death, his work is finished and he finds rest from his suffering. N. T. Wright says,

> Just as the creation story ended in triumph when God finished on the sixth day all the word he had understaken, and rested on the seven day (Genesis 23:1–3), so the last word of Jesus in John's

gospel is just that: "Finished!" (19:30). On the Friday morning, the sixth day of the week, Pilate brought out the man who was God incarnate; on the Friday afternoon God incarnate finished the work he had undertaken. And on the seventh day God incarnate rested in the tomb, rested from his completed labour. *The Word became flesh, and slept among us; we beheld his glory, glory as of the loving God who has finished the work of redemption.*[3]

This concept directly relates to the believer's Sabbath rest in salvation precisely in the sense that Jesus' saving work is complete. There is nothing lacking in God's salvation through Jesus.

What is the significance of this, then, for believers? This means that there is no more striving, or good works that need done in order for God's salvation to be complete. *There is nothing we can do to add to what Christ has done to bring about God's saving work in the world. It is finished.* We can rest from our efforts to earn God's favor because Christ has done it *all;* but what of the command to do good works that we find in the Scriptures? These good works are joyful acts of obedience. To obey God in our lives is the equivalent of a thanksgiving offering that we read about in the Old Testament sacrificial system. These works are not to earn or even prove our salvation. No, they are done out of joyful love.

REST FROM WRESTLING

This leads us to the third and final type of rest for believers and that is rest from wresting with the old sin nature. The Bible is very clear on the fact that sinning isn't the problem. Rather, the *sin nature* is the problem. Martin Luther described the sin nature by describing the individual as being "curved inward upon itself" (Latin, *incurvates in se*). Curved inward indeed! But what does this mean? This means that it is natural for people to *love themselves and see to their own interests first.* Not only this, but it also means seeing others as a threat to the well-being of the self and as a means for reaching self-centered goals. People, and even God himself, become mere instruments serving the purpose of the self. This is our natural state. This means that this is how we are when gone unchecked. This describes the character of humanity as it stands untouched by eternal influences. Hair grows without us having to try to make it grow (at least for most of us). In much the same way, we prioritize ourselves and our own needs over and

3. Wright, *Following Jesus,* 33.

above the needs of others without trying. It just is this way. This is the sin *nature*. Martin Luther explains this concept a bit further with this:

> The "prudence of the flesh" chooses what is good for oneself and avoids what is disadvantageous for oneself, it rejects the common good and chooses what is harmful to community. This is a prudence which directs the flesh, that is, our concupiscence and self-will, which enjoys itself and uses everyone else, including God Himself; in all matters it looks out for itself and its own interests. This prudence makes man feel that he himself is the final and ultimate object in life, and idol, on whose account he does, suffers, attempts, plans, and says all things. He considers good only those things that are for his own personal good, and those things only as evils which are bad for him. This crookedness, this depravity, this iniquity is condemned over and over in Scripture under the name of fornication and idolatry, and it is, as we have said early in chapter 6:12 something most profound in our nature, indeed, it is our very nature itself, wounded and totally in ferment, so that without grace it becomes not only incurable but also totally unrecognizable.[4]

The moral conscious (which is activated by God's grace so humanity doesn't annihilate itself) recognizes this problem. So much so that we build rules and boundaries around our societies that regulate the sort of behavior that is the result of people being curved inward on themselves. The Ten Commandments are the preeminent example. Why do we have to be told not to steal, not to commit adultery, not to covet, not to murder, etc.? It is because it's natural to do those things!

Do you know what happens when we try to regulate the sin nature with rules and a list of do's and don'ts? The sin nature rears its ugly head. The rules that seek to regulate and minimize the broad-sweeping damage that is caused by sinful people attempt to pin down the ugliness inside of us. The image that we get then is our "good self" that is in tune with a moral conscious to the fact that such behavior is bad, that is constantly wrestling with our "bad self." There is a constant struggle that happens between us wanting to do what is good and wanting to appease our carnal appetites. This is what Paul is talking about in Romans 7. Let me tell you, this struggle, this wrestling with the sin nature, is utterly *exhausting*. It's exhausting because we cannot win, we cannot beat it. It wins every time. What's ironic is that oftentimes even the acknowledgement of good and

4. Luther, *Lectures on Romans*, 350.

the attempt at piety and virtue itself becomes a means for self-service. This is self-righteousness—where all of our "good works" become a source of pride and arrogance that we then leverage against our fellow humans to get what we want. We use this to manipulate circumstances to serve our own needs. This is what happened to those who killed Jesus, by the way.

We have good news today. Through Jesus, we can rest from this battling. Through the death of Christ, the "old sinful man" (Rom 6:6) can be put to death once and for all. We can rest in Jesus through the indwelling of the Holy Spirit and in cooperation with the Holy Spirit, replace all of our old habits that were formed out of sin nature with the holy habits of Jesus; habits driven by love for others—habits driven by compassion, joy and peace. The exhaustion that comes from vainly battling the sin nature inside of us will only die when we die because we are *one with it*. We must die to ourselves. That's what this means. We must take up our cross. This is one of the greatest features of resting in Jesus.

This is the theological concept in the sign of baptism. In the symbol of baptism we die to our sinful selves (the sin nature) and resurrect with Jesus and take on *his character*. Baptism, then, is a sign of submission to kill the sin nature.

This means that the effects of the cross must be two-dimensional. In one sense, the cross takes away the guilt that we have incurred because of sinning. This is what we mean when we say that Jesus' blood washes away our sins. We no longer carry the stain of sin nor the guilt and shame that goes along with it. This is the dimension that gets all the attention when we talk about what Jesus and the cross does for believers. The other dimension gets neglected. That dimension is the dimension of the *sin nature*. You see, the death of Jesus not only washes away our sin-guilt, but it also puts to death our very sin nature. This is the part of the Good News of Jesus Christ that too often gets overlooked. The Enemy likes when we overlook it because it makes us live in a place where we say, "Oh well, I'm human, I'll always be a sinner." By no means! The power of the cross is rendered void if this is the case. The entire point of Jesus' life, death, and resurrection was to put to death the sin nature; to put an end to the fact that we are curved inward on ourselves.

SOME QUESTIONS TO CONSIDER

1. Is living the Christian life a constant struggle for you? Do you think it should be?

2. Do you have a strong tendency to solve your own problems, consulting God only as a last resort?

3. Do you believe that you can really rest in him, give him your problems and make him your first priority?

A GOSPEL SONG FOR MEDITATION

Following conversion, believers frequently encounter the contradiction of wanting to serve God with all their heart and mind but feel pulled by the influence of sin to do something totally different, a dilemma that is well stated in Romans 7. Eugene Peterson begins chapter 8 of Romans with this paraphrase of verses 1, "With the arrival of Jesus, the Messiah, *that fateful dilemma is resolved . . .*" (emphasis added).

Bill and Gloria Gaither expressed it well in their song, "It is Finished."

> There's a line that is drawn through the ages. On that line stands an old rugged cross.
>
> On that cross, a battle is raging. For the gain of man's soul or its loss. On one side, march the forces of evil, All the demons, all the devils of hell. On the other, the angels of glory, and they meet on Golgotha's hill. The earth shakes with the force of the conflict. And the sun refuses to shine. For there hangs God's son, in the balance. And then through the darkness he cries,
>
> It is finished, the battle is over. It is finished, there'll be no more war. It is finished, the end of the conflict. It is finished and Jesus is Lord.
>
> Yet in my heart, the battle was still raging. Not all prisoners of war had come home. These were battlefields of my own making. I didn't know that the war had been won. Oh, but then I heard the king of the ages, Had fought all the battles for me And that victory was mine for the claiming, And now praise his name, I am free.

10

LIFE

I came that they may have life, and have it abundantly. —John 10:10

Bondage to sin yields no return except shame and ongoing moral deterioration culminating in the death we deserve. Bondage to God, however, yields the precious fruit of progressive holiness, culminating in the free gift of life. —John R. W. Stott, *Message of Romans*

An American newspaper editor described Americans as being part of that strange race of people who spend their lives working at jobs they detest, to make money to buy things they don't need, to impress people they don't like.

Such a view of life would cause one to join the writer of Ecclesiastes in exclaiming, "Meaningless! Meaningless! Everything is meaningless. What does a man gain from all his labor?" (Eccl 1:2, NIV).

When one reads Christ's purpose statement in John 10:10, he may wrestle with reconciling that statement with other statements made by him, such as, "in this world you will have trouble" (John 16:33, NIV), "a man's enemies will be the members of his own household" (Matt 10:36, NIV), "treasures can rust, be stolen and destroyed" (Matt 5:19, NIV), and "there will be wars and rumors of war; famines, earthquakes, and persecution (Matt 26:6, NIV).

It seems like Jesus could echo the familiar words, "I Never Promised You a Rose Garden." We know the words from a semi-autobiographical novel by Joanne Greenberg, written in 1964 under the pen name of Hannah Green and made into a film in 1977 and a play in 2004. *I Never Promised You a Rose Garden* was also used by Joe South in the song, most famously recorded by Lynn Anderson in 1970.

The novel is a semi-autobiographical account of a teenage girl's three-year battle with schizophrenia. The closing statement of the novel is, "The rose-garden world of perfection is a lie . . . and a bore too." That may be true to some but Christ's promise of abundant living should not be discarded.

Epicurus, an ancient Greek philosopher, believed the purpose of philosophy was to attain the happy, tranquil life characterized by peace and freedom from fear, the absence of pain and by living a self-sufficient life surrounded by friends. He taught that pleasure and pain are the measures of what is good and evil; death is the end of both body and soul and should, therefore, not be feared. Although his philosophy has never been widely accepted nor propagated, it provides an excellent paradigm for what Jesus really promised about the life he came to give.

PEACE

Peace was a predominate ingredient of his promise of life. John 14:27 and 16:33 say it well:

> Peace, I leave with you; my peace I give you. I do not give to you as the world gives. Do not let your hearts be troubled and do not be afraid.

> I have told you these things so that in me you may have peace. In this world you will have trouble. But take heart! I have overcome the world.

While serving as homeland missionaries my wife and I (Charles) excitedly awaited the birth of our first child. We had learned that our new arrival was to be a girl and the expected date was set. With a busy travel schedule, I arranged to have a month off to get acquainted with my new daughter following her birth. My wife, however, did not cooperate and was two weeks late in delivering our new bundle of joy.

The first two weeks of her new life were joyful. I couldn't get enough of her antics and responses to my attention. Soon the day came when I needed to be back on the trail, traveling on behalf of the mission. My first assignment was to be more than 1200 miles away from home where I would speak for ten days in a family camp.

One night during the camp, a knock came on the door of my cabin. "You have an emergency phone call from your wife," was the message I heard. Walking to the phone I grew anxious to know the nature of the emergency. Our newborn daughter was in the hospital under an oxygen tent with a rare respiratory infection. The next twenty-four hours was the critical period that could ultimately determine life or death for our little child. Being twelve hundred miles away from home meant there was no way I could get there before the critical period was over.

I returned to my cabin needing to speak to the camp within fifteen minutes. I did the only thing I knew to do. I repeated a lesson taught to me by my mother in my childhood. When there's nothing you can humanly do to resolve a problem, give it over to the Lord and tell him you will praise him whatever the outcome. That night I got on my knees and prayed a simple but very difficult prayer, "Lord, I put my wife and little daughter into your hands. Heal my daughter and let her live and I will praise you. If you choose not to, I will praise you still."

I couldn't believe the overwhelming peace that came to me in that moment. I went to the service and spoke with the anointing of the Lord. I told no one of this crisis until after the service. I slept well that night and rejoiced the next day when a mid-morning call came to assure me the crisis had past and our daughter was on her way to recovery.

The peace of Christ is not the promise of the absence of turmoil but peace in the midst of it. His peace, an inner peace, comes through faith, which gives us access to the grace of God and hope in the midst of suffering. We, therefore, have peace and rejoice in our sufferings. That peace comes from our right relationship with Christ and our complete surrender to him.

FREEDOM FROM FEAR

In Christ, we have freedom from fear. In Hebrews 2:14–15 we are told that Christ took on flesh that by his death he might destroy him who holds the power of death—that is the devil—and free those who all their lives were held in slavery by their fear of death.

John tells us that God is love.

Whoever lives in love lives in God, and God in him. In this way love is made complete among us so that we will have confidence on the day of judgment. There is no fear in love. But perfect love drives out fear, because fear has to do with punishment. The one who fears is not made perfect in love. (1 John 4:16–18, NIV)

PAIN

Two men in the same congregation were victims of severe pain; one from an incurable disease, the other from a tragic accident. Upon his first visit to the men in the hospital, the pastor discovered two totally different responses. One cursed his pain while the other declared to have become a friend to pain until the will of God was manifested in his body. The one who cursed his pain was later discharged from the hospital and battled with his pain until, one day, he felt he could bear it no longer and after leaving his wife and family a note, took his own life, bringing grief and pain to those who loved him.

The other assured the pastor of his faith in the time of pain. "God has not promised me a life without pain but has promised grace to see me through it," he affirmed. He shared his love for Andre Crouch's song, *Through It All*. Especially the words, "I've learned to trust in Jesus, I've learned to trust in God." Paul's thorn in the flesh was another passage he treasured. "If the grace of God was sufficient for Paul, it should be sufficient for me," he claimed. He was never freed from his pain and several years later died of lasting complications from his accident.

The witness of his life that stood out from all others was the victory over pain his friends saw him display. Even in his pain he ministered to others going through similar situations. He seldom complained and frequently was heard praising God for giving him added days to his life to enjoy family and friends. His walk with the Lord was unquestionable and his witness of Christ led others to know Christ as well.

The absence of pain is not a part of Christ's promise but in the presence of pain his presence brings comfort. He promises not to allow us to suffer beyond our ability to cope and promises that his grace will be sufficient for us as we depend on him. Today's emphasis on assisted suicides is a slap in the face to God's promise and a selfish attitude that betrays the sufficiency of God's grace.

Living a self-sufficient life is just the opposite of a holy life. A holy lifestyle is lived in total dependency not self-sufficiency. Self-sufficiency is presumption. Dependency is the key to vitality.

> Such confidence as this is ours through Christ before God. Not that we are competent in ourselves to claim anything for ourselves but our competence comes from God. He has made us competent. . . (2 Cor 3:4–6a, NIV)

PLEASURE

The measure of what is good is not measured by pleasure. Jesus made it clear to his audience that *man's life consists not in the things a man possesses.* Sin is pleasurable but only temporarily. "He who loves pleasure will become poor" (Prov 21:17, NIV). Pleasure, in and of itself, is not evil. Something is pleasurable to the degree that it pleases the one seeking it. The person committed to living a holy life is not seeking pleasure but that which is pleasing to God and in pleasing God finds true pleasure.

Recently, a young contestant on a TV reality show spoke of his beloved family and how he cherished his godly parents and the contribution they had made to his life. His concluding comment caught the attention of millions, "My family was rich in everything but money."

A fulfilling lifestyle does not guarantee a rose garden. Christ's promise for an abundant life embraces a realistic view of living, a realism that can be witnessed in Paul's comments, "hard pressed on every side, but not crushed; perplexed but not in despair; persecuted, but not abandoned; struck down, but not destroyed" (2 Cor 4:8–9, NIV). Never crushed, never left in despair, never abandoned and never destroyed are awesome components of an abundant life. A holy lifestyle does not guarantee a life without temptation and testing.

Yielding to the Lordship of Christ does not make one mature, let alone perfect. As long as we are human we will learn to live with our human limitations. The Spirit-filled Christian:

1. **Is still capable of sinning.** He is capable of identifying involuntary feelings and impulses and thoughts for what they are—temptations. He will rebuke the enemy and not submit, remembering that temptation is not sin. He will still have the capacity to choose, to yield to sin as Adam did. Yielding will generally occur when his disciplines are

lacking. Failure to live in the Word, prayer and the daily surrender of one's self to the Lord weakens one's resistance to sin. He will, however, be more sensitive to sin and desirous of repenting when sin is made known by the Holy Spirit (1 Cor 9.27; 10:12, 13; 1 John 1:9; 2:1; all imply the possibility of sinning).

2. **Is still finite in judgment.** A Spirit-led believer is still capable of making wrong choices on the basis of incomplete or inadequate knowledge. He is capable of doing the wrong thing with the right motive but less capable of doing the right thing for the wrong motive, his heart made pure by the Spirit. The Spirit purifies his motives. He can still fail a test, go bankrupt, have an automobile accident, etc.

3. **Still may have damaged emotions.** He may suffer from a poor self-concept; demonstrate perfectionistic tendencies. He may wrestle with periodic depression. Even Charles Spurgeon, one of England's greatest preachers, once said, "I am the subject of depressions of spirit so fearful that I hope none of you ever get to such extremes of wretchedness as I go to." What appears to be egotism, self-centeredness in some Spirit-filled Christians may be compensation for deep feelings of insecurity and lack of self-worth. Spirit-filled believers will not, however, use these as an excuse for sin but will seek the presence of the Holy Spirit in life to grow and overcome such weaknesses.

4. **Will still show signs of immaturity.** Purity is not maturity! The fruit of the Spirit will be evident in differing degrees. Fruit takes time to ripen. In Romans 7:17 Paul comments, "it is no longer I who do it, but sin that dwells within me." Yet in Galatians 2:20 his tone has changed when he comments, "I no longer live—but Christ lives in me" (NIV).

The benefits of Spirit-filled living lay in the believer's strengths that result from his yieldedness to the Spirit's power. In Christ, he:

1. **Has greater power over temptation.** With a new nature exchanged for the old, he no longer has a self-centered will to which to appeal. Our bent to sinning having been cleansed, the Adversary has only the believer's Christ-centered will to which to aim his schemes. With that will surrendered to the will of God, the Devil confronts a near impossible task. Purity of heart has been defined *to will one will*. Wholly and totally his, the Spirit-filled believer lives to please the Lord by keeping his life free from willful sin (1 Cor 10:13; John 14:30–31).

2. **Exercises greater spiritual discernment**. Having the mind of Christ, the believer seeks to have his mind renewed to think God's thoughts and know God's will. Discerning the mind of the Spirit is more important in a Spirit-filled believer's life as he is committed to minding the things of the Spirit (Rom 8:5; 1 Cor 2:9–10, 15–16).

3. **Realizes increased growth in personal holiness**. The sanctifying process of the Spirit having begun, the believer sets himself to *work out* what Christ has *worked in* his heart. The phrases "put off" and "put on" become practical goals. He considers the place of the basic Christian disciplines being exercised in his life. *Living on the cutting edge*, he allows the Holy Spirit to take the initiative of transforming and maturing his faith (1 Thess 5:23, 24; 1 Tim 4:7–8; Phil 2:12, 13).

4. **Experiences an anointing upon his ministry**. The promise of power was always associated with the indwelling fullness of the Spirit, power to be and to do. The power is embodied in his presence. Going into the world to proclaim his redemption, the believer has the guarantee of his presence and his power assuring constant victory as the believer trusts in him and not in himself (2 Cor 4:7, 16; Acts 1:8; 1 John 2:20–27).

5. **Demonstrates greater love in human relationships**. A pure heart and a separated life demonstrate itself in human relationships. The Corinthian believers, carnal as they were, could not live at peace with one another. They treated each other with contempt and were divisive.

Many of the biblical admonitions regarding the Holy Spirit are in the context of human relationships. How does one *grieve* the Holy Spirit? By speaking unkind words to another. Wesley's favorite phrase to denote a Spirit-filled life was "perfect love." Perfected in love, the believer speaks and acts because he loves. Love is the prevailing motivation of his life. He did not speak of absolute perfection but perfection of motive (Heb 12:14; Eph 4:29–32).

Having realistic expectations about life is important to any human being. The Spirit-filled life is a rose garden but not without thorns. God has a way of using even the thorns to bring joy and abundance to a believer's life.

WHAT DOES A HOLY LIFESTYLE LOOK LIKE?

Holy Living: The Standard

> Since everything will be destroyed in this way (by fire), what kind of people ought you to be? You ought to live holy and godly lives as you look forward to the day of God and speed His coming. (2 Pet 3:11, NIV)

1. **Holy in all manner of life**. "But as he who has called you is holy, so be ye holy in all manner of conversation (in all you do); because it is written, Be ye holy; for I am holy" (1 Pet 1:15, 16, KJV).

2. **Holy in human relationships**. "Make every effort to live in peace with all men and to be holy; without holiness no one will see the Lord. See to it that no one misses the grace of God and that no bitter root grows up to cause trouble and defile many" (Heb 12:14–15, NIV).

3. **Holy in control of one's body**. "It is God's will that you should be sanctified; that you should avoid sexual immorality; that each of you should learn to control his own body in a way that is holy and honorable, not in passionate lust like the heathen who do not know God . . . For God did not call us to be impure, but to live a holy life" (1 Thess 4:3–8; Eph 5:3, NIV).

4. **Holy in verbal communication**. "Speaking of things improper for God's holy people. Nor should there be obscenity, foolish talk or coarse joking, which are out of place but rather thanksgiving" (Eph 5:3–5, NIV).

5. **Holy in the focus of your mind**. "Finally, brothers, whatever is true, noble, right, pure, lovely, admirable, if anything is excellent or praise worthy—think about such things" (Phil 4:8; 2 Cor 10:5, NIV).

If you want to be a Christian, of course you'll repent of your sins. But after you've repented of your sins, you'll have to repent of how you have used the good things in your life to fill the place where God should have been. If you want intimacy with God and if you want to get over this sense that something is missing, it will have to become God that you love with all your heart and strength.

SOME QUESTIONS TO CONSIDER

1. Do you consider yourself experiencing the abundant life Christ came to give? If not, why not?

2. Have you ever experienced peace in the midst of a crisis, knowing that God was in control and would ultimately use that crisis for your good and his glory?

3. What is the most severe pain you ever experienced? How did you respond to it?

4. What did you learn from it?

5. Pleasure is not all bad. What part does it play in your life?

6. Why would you recommend life in Christ to someone else?

A GOSPEL SONG FOR MEDITATION: HE ABIDES

I'm rejoicing night and day, As I walk the narrow way, For the hand of God in all my life I see; And the reason of my bliss, Yes, the secret all is this: That the Comforter abides with me.

Refrain: He abides, He abides; Hallelujah, He abides with me! I'm rejoicing night and day, As I walk the narrow way, For the Comforter abides with me.

Once my heart was full of sin, Once I had no peace within, Till I heard how Jesus died upon the tree; Then I fell down at His feet, And there came a peace so sweet; Now the Comforter abides with me.

He is with me everywhere, And He knows my every care; I'm as happy as a bird and just as free; For the Spirit has control; Jesus satisfies my soul, Since the Comforter abides with me.

There's no thirsting for the things, Of the world—they've taken wings; Long ago I gave them up, and instantly, All my night was turned to day, All my burdens rolled away; Now the Comforter abides with me.

Author Herbert Buffum was born November 13, 1879, in Lafayette, Illinois, and died October 9, 1939, in Los Angeles, California. After moving with his family to California and being converted to Christ at age eighteen,

Buffum felt a call to the ministry. He held ministerial credentials with the Church of the Nazarene and was a prolific songwriter, with many of his songs inspired by personal experience.

11

SENT

Peace be with you! As the Father has sent me, I am sending you. And with that he
breathed on them and said, "Receive the Holy Spirit." —John 20:21–22, NIV

There is no holiness without social holiness. —John Wesley

In our era, the road to holiness necessarily passes through the world of action.
—Dag Hammarskjold, *Markings*

The holy life is a life of balance and conjunction. It joins a clear head
and warm heart; the emotion and the substance; and the inner life of
devotion and outer life of ministry; the spiritual and the social.

The cross has two beams: one vertical (our relationship to God), and
one horizontal (our relationship to one another). Holiness without concern
is a soul without a body. Social concern without holiness is a body without
a soul. One is a ghost, the other a corpse. Only when they are wedded together do we have a living organism.

A number of four-letter words join the word "send" to enlarge the
purpose for God's making people holy; "lose," "care," "feed," "give," "work."
Consider the usage of the words in Scripture.

THE PARADOX OF LOSING

> Whoever finds his life will lose it, and whoever loses his life for my sake will find it. (Matt 10:39)

The verse is spoken in the context of *losing* one's life in service to others.

An older pastor, mentoring two young pastors just beginning their pastoral ministry, commented on the recent death of George Beverly Shea. "Who's he?" one of them asked. Surprised, the elder pastor asked a question in return, "You do know who Billy Graham is, don't you?" They did. Dr. Graham's name will be remembered long after he's gone to glory. Another name the world will long remember is Mother Teresa of Calcutta. An interesting contrast, isn't it? Dr. Graham known for his lifetime commitment to evangelism and Mother Teresa's lifetime commitment to social action.

Look for someone who lost her life to find it and you'll find the picture of Mother Teresa. Of Albanian origin, she lived most of her life in India. She founded the Missionaries of Charity, which in 2012 consisted of over 4,500 sisters and ministry in 133 countries. She was the 1979 recipient of the Nobel Peace Prize. She lost her life ministering to HIV/AIDS victims, lepers, TB sufferers, orphans, and the list goes on. She did it all in the name of Christ.

> A controversial figure both during her life and after her death in 1997, Mother Teresa was widely admired by many for her charitable works, but also widely criticized, particularly for her campaigns against contraception and for substandard conditions in the hospices for which she was responsible.[1]

Mother Teresa never let criticism daunt her efforts. She modeled the love of Christ to a world in need.

In Christ's conversation with Peter following the resurrection, Jesus told Peter that if he truly loved him he would *care* for of his sheep. The adage is true: "People don't care how much you know until they know how much you care."

Google the name "Clara" and Clara Barton will be the first to emerge. Born in 1821 and died in 1912, Clara Barton was the pioneer nurse that founded the American Red Cross. Sacrificing opportunities to marry, Clara began her ministry of caring by creating a hospital where she ministered

---

1. *Wikipedia*, s.v. "Mother Teresa."

to prisoners in the prison camp at Andersonville during the Civil War. Following the war, the American Red Cross responded to such crises as earthquakes, forest fires, and hurricanes. Interestingly, Clara died at the age of ninety, after suffering for two years with tuberculosis, a disease she had helped fight for a long number of years.

Although not a professed Christian, Clara exemplified a Christ-like caring for people in need. A self-described universalist, she ministered to the needs of hurting people through an organization that stills lives in her memory and sets an example worthy to be followed.

"Feed" is used both in the previously mentioned verse as well as in Romans 12:20 where Paul admonishes us, "If your enemy is hungry, feed him; if he is thirsty, give him something to drink." The words of Jesus are sobering when he said to his disciples, "I was hungry and you gave me something to eat," and later clarified his statement to his puzzled followers, "Inasmuch as you have done it unto one of the least of these, you have done it unto me."

The feeding of sheep is a common biblical concept. When Jesus communicated with Peter about caring for his sheep, twice he used the command to feed them. In 1 Peter 5:2, Peter admonishes the elders of the church to feed the flock placed under their care. Talk with a sheep farmer and you can learn a number of general recommendations for adequate feeding. Among them might be, forage should provide the majority of nutrients for the sheep, proper feeding requires more than one pen or pasture, and it's good to start by feeding a smaller amount of grain per day and gradually increase the level.

Whether the feeding of believers is being done by a pastor, a small group leader or even self-feeding the Word of God, it should provide the majority of spiritual nutrients. Other places beside the sanctuary of the church are needed to adequately feed them, and a proper diet for a new believer is lighter than that for a maturing one. Believers who busy themselves in the *feeding* ministry serve in obedience to Christ's heart and desire that believers grow.

Often, however, the need for the feeding of the hungry is a physical need. "Will work for food" is a recurring sight on a cardboard sign being held by a man or woman standing on an American street corner. Believers must remember that not even a cup of cold water given in Jesus' name will go unrewarded. Soup kitchens abound and the need for volunteers to help in the serving of the food is always great. Christian businessmen and women in the food industry can contribute greatly to the need as they carefully steward the leftovers or the damaged containers that are often discarded.

Jesus reminded his disciples in the Sermon the Mount, "When you give to the needy, do not let your left hand know what your right hand is doing" (Matt 6:3, NIV).

A medical doctor who had a heart for the less fortunate sought ways to meet the needs of those around him. The Lord revealed to him a plan which he humbly accepted and lived his life to fulfill. Knowing that his regular pay would be more than he and his family would need, he determined a salary that would be adequate for them and then promised God that everything he made over that amount he would give to help those less fortunate. He even witnessed to the fact that he prayed that God would help him make all the money he could make. With a fixed salary, increased income would simply mean more to give to those in need. Generously he gave and generously he received.

The possibilities of rendering good deeds are more numerous than the sands of the sea. One does not have to look very far to find ways to better the lives of others, especially those whose resources are less than his own. An Atlanta television station daily sets the example by rendering a *random act of kindness* asking only that in return, the recipient seek ways to reciprocate by rendering kindness to someone in his sphere of influence. Spice is added to life when one looks daily for opportunity to do an act of kindness to someone in need. After all, we are saved to render the works God intended for us, even before we came to know him.

The role of work in the life of a Christ-follower is made very clear in Ephesians 2:8–10:

> For by grace you have been saved through faith. And this is not your own doing; it is the gift of God, not a result of works, so that no one may boast. For we are his workmanship, created in Christ Jesus for good works, which God prepared beforehand, that we should walk in them. Therefore remember that at one time you Gentiles in the flesh, called "the uncircumcision" by what is called the circumcision, which is made in the flesh by hands.

THE COMPASSIONATE CHRIST

One of the predominant characteristics of our Lord is that of his compassion. When he saw the crowds, he had compassion on them (Matt 9:36) .An interesting story in Mark chapter 8 is the account of Christ healing a blind man at Bethsaida. It is the only record of a healing, which Christ performed in two steps. After his initial touch, the man saw people looking like trees walking. After his second touch, his eyes were opened, his sight was restored, and he saw everything clearly (v. 25).

Bible scholars have debated the meaning of the healing. It would make sense to see it as a miracle Christ used as a parable to teach his disciples a simple lesson. God sees people differently than man sees people. We tend to put people into categories: the rich and the poor, the educated and the uneducated, Jews and Gentiles, nationals and foreigners, etc. God has a way of seeing all mankind alike. "There is neither Jew nor Greek, slave nor free, male nor female, for you are all one in Christ Jesus" (Gal 3:28, NIV).

Compassion becomes a quality in a believer's life when he sees people as Christ sees them. What a difference it would make if we saw every human being as an object of God's creation, made in his own image:

- a soul for whom Christ died, thus, a person of infinite value

- an individual bound for eternity to someday stand before the judge of the universe. In Ephesians 4:11 Paul says that pastors and teachers are given to the church "to prepare God's people for works of service." It would stand to reason that God has work for us to do. Believers who discover their ministry find a level of fulfillment in life that cannot be found anywhere else.

For some believers it may mean pioneering a new ministry. For others, it may mean joining a ministry already initiated. God has a work for each to do.

THE LACK OF COMPASSION IN TODAY'S CHURCH

America, has entered a dark and deceptive period of selfishness in our culture and our political life. "I" has replaced "we." Possessing is more important than sharing and that hinders finding solutions to real and growing problems in our country and our world.

One of the crises facing today's church is individualism: the belief that we can do our own thing. Our culture is *radically* individualistic. People do whatever they want when they want to do it. People in our churches are not necessarily different. They, too, continue to be radically individualistic, never dealing with the issue of their own self-centered existence. They pick and choose churches where they will attend, believe what they want, and fail to ever understand the responsibilities of being part of a family of believers with a mandate from God to "go into all the world."

Many people sitting in the pews have missed the whole point and need to get in touch with reality. Jesus was concerned for the hungry, the naked, the homeless, the imprisoned, the orphaned, the widowed, the immigrant, and those who suffer injustice. James negated the genuineness of our Christian experience if we neglect those in need around us. James reminds us that "religion that is pure and undefiled before God, the Father, is this: to visit orphans and widows in their affliction, and to keep oneself unstained from the world" (1:27).

Consider a Christian who devotes his life to God but lives an average life doing nothing to change his world substantially. Then consider an atheist who devotes his life to humanitarian causes changing the world substantially in a positive way but has no place for God in his life. Which is worse? Obviously, the call for balance is essential. The humanitarian may change the conditions surrounding a man and have little or no effect on his inner condition. The compassionate Christian can, through the power of the Holy Spirit, affect both.

THE CALL FOR BALANCE

Holiness without social concern is, indeed, a soul without a body. Holy living and social concern is a divine balance needed in our world and our churches today.

The writer of Hebrews gives an encouraging word regarding our work, God is not unjust; he will not forget your work and the love you have shown him as you have helped his people and continue to help them (Heb 6:10).

There is no more sobering parable in the Bible than the parable of the sheep and the goats, recorded in Matthew 25:31–46. The Son of Man is pictured seated on his throne of judgment with all the nations of the earth before him. He proceeds by separating the people "as a shepherd separates the sheep from the goats." The issue? Feeding the hungry, giving drink to the thirsty, taking in the stranger, clothing the naked, and visiting the sick and imprisoned.

To those on his left, Jesus accused them of failure to do each of those ministries to him. They were dumbfounded. Never had they seen him as a hungry, thirsty, stranger, needing clothes, sick or imprisoned. His response, "Inasmuch, as you did not do for one of the least of these, you did not do for me." In conclusion, "they went away to eternal punishment."

To the righteous, who likewise had failed to see Christ in the needy yet who ministered to them just the same, the conclusion was different . . . *the righteous to eternal life.*

The Salvation Army began in 1865 when William Booth, a London minister, gave up the comfort of his pulpit and decided to take his message into the streets where it would reach the poor, the homeless, the hungry and the destitute.

His original aim was to send converts to established churches of the day, but soon he realized that the poor did not feel comfortable or welcome in the pews of most of the churches and chapels of Victorian England. Regular churchgoers were appalled when these shabbily dressed, unwashed people came to join them in worship. Booth decided to found a church especially for them—the East London Christian Mission. The mission grew slowly, but Booth's faith in God remained undiminished.

In May 1878, Booth summoned his son, Bramwell, and his good friend, George Railton, to read a proof of the Christian Mission's annual report. At the top it read: "The Christian Mission is a Volunteer Army." Bramwell strongly objected to this wording. He was not a volunteer: he was compelled to do God's work. So, in a flash of inspiration, Booth crossed out "Volunteer" and wrote the word "Salvation." With this the Salvation Army was born. What Booth began over a hundred and thirty-five years ago continues today ministering to the "least of these." Few believers have ever lived who more realistically personified the balance between evangelism and social holiness.

The believer who has committed himself to put others before himself, who has lost his life to find it in Christ, who daily lives in response to the Spirit's promptings in this life, is a believer who makes a difference in his world.

A CHALLENGE

What do you do with the loose change in your pocket or purse? Try saving it for a while. Allow it to accumulate up to $25 or $50. Then ask the Lord to direct you to someone who needs it. He will! Tell the person that someone instructred you to make it a gift. Evaluate the effect this simple act of kindness has on you.

Remember when an expert in the law asked Jesus what he must do to inherit eternal life and Jesus responded with, "Love the Lord your God with all your heart and with all your soul and with all your strength and with all your mind and love your neighbor as yourself." Christ's answer was responded to with another question, "Who is my neighbor?"

Interestingly, Jesus' answer did not describe the person who lived next door. Most readers will remember the parable of the Good Samaritan; the man who fell among thieves, the priest and the Levite who passed him by. But then came the Good Samaritan who had the same compassion toward him as the compassion Christ demonstrated when he saw people in need.

Possessing no racial biases, the Samaritan not only addressed his immediate need, he provided for his continued care.

Jesus then asked his inquirer, "Which of these three do you think was a neighbor? The man could not escape the obvious, the one who had mercy on him." Christ's response was timeless and speaks to us as much as it did to the expert in law, "Go and do likewise" (Luke 10:25–37, NIV). Be on the lookout for your neighbor.

SOME QUESTIONS TO CONSIDER

1. Can you say that you have lost your life to find it?

2. How long has it been since you cared for someone who needed caring for, fed someone who needed food, given to someone who had need, or rendered a random act of kindness to someone who needed your love?

3. In what ways are you out to change your world by making it a better place for someone to live?

A SPIRITUAL SONG FOR MEDITATION: REACH OUT AND TOUCH

Reach out and touch a soul that is hungry; Reach out and touch a spirit in despair; Reach out and touch a life torn and dirty, A man who is lonely—If you care! Reach out and touch that neighbor who hates you; Reach out and touch that stranger who meets you; Reach out and touch the brother who needs you; Reach out and let the smile of God touch thro' you. Reach out and touch a friend who is weary; Reach out and touch a seeker unaware; Reach out and touch tho' touching means losing A part of your own self—If you dare!

Reach out and give your love to the love-less; Reach out and make a home for the homeless; Reach out and shed God's light in the darkness; Reach out and let the smile of God touch thro' you.

—Charles F. Brown (1971)

12

―――――

CALL

For God did not call us to be impure, but to live a holy life. — 1 Thessalonians 4:7

The word "called" is most often used in the church in a very limited manner. Men and women are called into Christian service. The Bible, however, does not limit the word to a call to professional ministry. In Acts 11:26 the disciples were first called Christians at Antioch. In Galatians 5:1 Paul reminded the Galatian believers that they were called to be free from the yoke of slavery to the law. In 1 Corinthians 7:15 Paul stressed that we are called to live in peace. In 1 Peter 2:9 Peter describes conversion to Christ as having been called out of darkness into his wonderful light.

Each of those calls are challenging but none more so than the call in 1 Thessalonians 4:7 wherein God has called us to live a holy life. Thus, in the previous chapters, we have made an attempt to better understand what a holy life looks like. Hopefully, we have clarified some areas of misunderstanding.

In the opinion of the authors, three unfortunate words appear in the discussion and understanding of a holy lifestyle. They are "filled," "destroyed," and "perfection." The first, we have devoted a separate chapter to (see ch. 4). The second is based on one of the key texts of the Bible, Romans 6:6, which Chinese Christian Watchman Nee referred to as "The Gospel for

Christians." The third is known as John Wesley's favorite expression for the holy life.

Being *filled* with the Spirit, as we stated earlier, has nothing to do with quantity but everything to do with control. It's not a matter of how much of the Holy Spirit you have in you but how much of you the Holy Spirit controls. Living under the control of the Spirit is experiencing the Lordship of Christ. Every believer is indwelt by the Spirit and knows his baptism but many believers, as yet, have not experienced his fullness and known his ultimate power in their life.

WHAT HAPPENS TO OUR OLD NATURE?

In Romans 6:6 we are told that our old nature was crucified with Christ so that the body of sin might be ("destroyed," KJV), "done away with" (NIV), that we should no longer be slaves to sin—because anyone who has died has been freed from sin. The debate is over the use of the word "destroyed." Note that the verse does not say that a believer has simply been nailed to the cross but that he has *died to the old nature*. The Greek word is a strong one meaning to "to cleanse", "to put off", "to render inoperative", "to destroy".y. In the Greek, "suppression" and "destruction" are different than the word used here. Repression or restraint are not used or inferred in the passage.

One meaning of the word is "to cleanse," which means, "to change." Through our identification with Christ our old nature is changed from a self-centered existence to a Christ-centered life. The change affects our emotions, our wills and our motives, thus changing our behavior. We no longer live for ourselves but for God. Such a change of relationship can happen in response to a penitent heart seeking to know the Spirit's fullness through the total surrender to his Lordship.

John Wesley believed that closeness of relationship could be forfeited. Paul felt it necessary to "die daily" in order to maintain his surrender to Christ. The relationship is improvable. The believer can continue to grow in grace and allow the fruit of the Spirit to ripen in his life. The old nature can best be understood in terms of relationship rather than thingness; something that can be changed rather than destroyed. Human nature remains but the adjective *carnal* can be exchanged for *spiritual*.

On the heels of that concern, the issue of perfection is raised. Often a significant question is raised. If the old nature is destroyed, rendered inoperative, or even changed, does that mean that a believer can never sin again? Can we believe in sinless perfection? Definitely not!

W. E. Sangster (1900–1960), senior minister for sixteen years at Westminster Central Hall (*The Cathedral of Methodism* in England) in his book *The Pure in Heart* struggles with the question:

> Furthermore, the exponents of eradication, admitting (as they must) that some from whom they believed all sin to be eradicated had lapsed into grievous sin again, have never been able satisfactorily to explain where the sin came from that caused this second distressing fall. To say, as they do, that the person yielded to new temptation is inadequate. Sin takes hold on us because there is something in us on which it can take hold. If we are to give credence to the idea that from some natures 'the dire root' of sin has been entirely eradicated, on what did the new sin take hold.[1]

John R. W. Stott, in his commentary on the Epistle to the Romans, raises the same question. If our fallen nature were dead and had no desires, or if we had a "sanctified disposition" from which the inclination to sin had been removed, how could we be no longer responsive to temptation?

A significant answer can be given. When Adam first sinned, on what did sin take hold? Not on a nature that was carnal. He was made in the image of God. Sin had only his *free moral agency* to which to make its appeal. Man can never reach a place where he is no longer capable of responding to temptation. What then is the basic difference between the carnal Christian and the Spirit-filled Christian in the time of temptation?

The Spirit-filled life has little effect on the *quantity* of temptation in a believer's life. In fact, temptation may increase. But it does, however, have a great effect upon its *quality*. In the unsanctified heart the Adversary appeals to a carnal mind with its bent toward sinning. In the sanctified heart he appeals only to a person's will, and if that will is kept surrendered to Christ's Lordship, the Adversary has little chance to lead a believer into willful sin. A will totally yielded to the Lordship of Christ willing to yield to sin is a contradiction.

CAN WE REALLY BE MADE PERFECT?

"Perfection" is found frequently in the New Testament. It speaks, however, of a relative perfection not an absolute one. Only God is absolute perfection

1. Sangster, *Pure in Heart*, 228.

and someday we shall be like Christ, but not on this side of glory. John Wesley loved the term "Christian perfection." He spoke of man being made perfect in love, "loving God will all your heart, mind soul, and strength; and our neighbor as ourselves."

> For he chose us in him before the creation of the world to be holy and blameless in his sight. In love he predestined us to be adopted as his sons through Jesus Christ, in accordance with his pleasure and will—to the praise of his glorious grace which he has freely given us in the One he loves. (Eph 1:4–6, NIV)

When and how God makes us holy has always been a part of the discussion. We can resort to the tenses of verbs in the original language to debate whether it is a momentary, completed act or a continuous action, or both. We can resort to the traditional four basic positions on when he does it; concomitant or subsequent to salvation, progressively or at the hour of our death but two truths are very clear. It is the will of God that his people be holy and he has promised to sanctify his people. He desires to set us apart unto himself, to be exclusively his and, in a moral sense, make us pure, upright and holy, living daily in victory over willful and habitual sin.

God accomplished that ability through his Son on the cross. It must be obvious that what we are talking about is something the Father does, not something we can do for ourselves. Through faith in the finished work of Christ on Calvary we can experience a change of our inner nature. One who is sanctified is a partaker of God's divine nature. The old nature of sin is changed in the experience and process of sanctification and the divine nature or likeness of God is reinstated in the heart.

> That you put off concerning the former conversation the old man [carnal nature or sin principle] . . . And . . . put on the new man [divine nature], which after God is created in righteousness and true holiness. (Eph 4:24, KJV)

> You have put off the old man with his deeds [actual transgressions or committed sins] and have put on the new man which is renewed in knowledge after the image of him that created him. (Col 3:9b–10, KJV)

> But we all, with open face beholding as in a glass the glory of the Lord, are changed into the same image from glory to glory, even as by the Spirit of the Lord. (2 Cor 3:18, KJV)

Note that all these passages speak of a change of condition and nature in the believer. His divine power has given us everything we need for life and godliness through our knowledge of him who called us by his own glory and goodness. Through these he has given us his very great and precious promises, so that through them you may participate in the divine nature and escape the corruption in the world caused by evil desires (2 Pet 1:3–4).

Drew grew up in a Christian home. Mom and Dad were not only professing Christians, they were devoted to living out their faith in practical ways. During the summer months they were faithful attenders to a nearby holiness camp meeting. The word "holiness" presented something of a stigma to Drew because among his peers, it had very negative connotations. To talk about holiness was to talk about a legalism which manifested itself in holding to certain doctrines, dress, and a list of dos and don'ts which, to him, ruled out having any fun in life.

Drew attended the camps, however, and listened carefully to the messages as they were presented. He was quite analytical and needed an answer for every question before he accepted anything to be true. When he raised questions, it seemed to him that he was immediately put on someone's prayer list without securing any reasonable answer to his inquiry.

His college years took him away from a Christian environment but not away from the longing to understand the logic of his upbringing and faith to which he had been so fully exposed. During the summer months he even agreed to visit the camp meeting during the week when he wasn't working. His confusion, however, only deepened.

At the university he faithfully attended the campus chapter of Inter-Varsity and felt he was growing in his faith. There was, however, something missing. He believed there was something more for him but sought vigorously in vain to find it. Some of his peers were attached to a charismatic group at a local church near the campus. Sharing his quest for something more, they suggested that he needed to be baptized in the Spirit. He had already explored that subject thoroughly and was firmly fixed in his understanding of the biblical basis for his belief that he was baptized in the Spirit when he was born anew in Christ.

Drew believed that every believer was baptized in the Spirit when they chose to follow Christ. A thorough study of the gifts of the Spirit led him to not only believe in the gifts mentioned in God's Word but also believe that every gift was not ordained for every believer, thus no one gift could be singled out as the evidence of the Spirit's baptism. He did not sit in judgment on his friends who believed otherwise but failed to find any consolation in their suggested remedy.

He graduated from the university, married his high school sweetheart, and settled into a home believing that he must have experienced all there was for him to experience. Living the Christian life in his workplace was a challenge but, apart from an occasional stumble, he remained faithful to commitment to Christ.

Drew later found himself passing through a significant crisis. He leaned heavily upon his faith to see him through it but it didn't seem enough. Reawakened in his heart was the feeling of incompleteness and his desire for something more. He cried out to God in desperation. His prayer was rather simple, "Lord, I need something more. I give you all I have. Give me all you have for me. I can't explain my request in theological terms but rest my case before you."

Something happened in Drew's life that he could not fully explain. However, as the weeks progressed and victory in his crisis was evident, Drew began to read the Word of God in a new light. His understanding increased and issues that were once foggy were made clear. Written resources came unexpectedly into his possession and answers were found to the haunting questions he had asked for so long.

Later, a Christian brother shared with him what he believed was God's call upon his life for him and his wife to go overseas as missionaries. The brother asked of Drew, "Have you ever felt God calling you to anything?" Drew responded, "I always made myself available to God for whatever he wanted me to do, but the only call I have never been able to escape is the call to live a holy life."

Consider yourself among the called of God. The Lord commands us, "Be holy as I am Holy." If he commands it, then it must be possible! Such a lifestyle is attainable and we can only pray that through the reading of this book you can better understand how a holy life is attained. Experiences of believers will inevitably differ. He wills, however, that we be transformed to the image of God and be holy as he is holy. His call is inclusive and no believer is exempt.

SOME QUESTIONS TO CONSIDER

1. Have you ever had the feeling that God had something more for you? How have you opened yourself to that possibility?

2. We do not base our belief on our experience. We test our experience by our belief in the Word of God. Belief often comes as a result of our seeking truth from the Word and then our obedience to what we discover. How do you consider that?

3. Do you daily sense God's call to a holy life? Is there any un-surrendered area of your life, which would prevent you from living a holy lifestyle? What is it?

4. Have you experienced an increase in understanding the Word of God as a result of a deeper commitment to Christ? How?

OUR PRAYER FOR YOU

May God himself, the God of peace, sanctify you through and through. May your whole spirit, soul and body be kept blameless at the coming of our Lord Jesus Christ. The one who calls you is faithful and he will do it. (1 Thess 5:23–24, NIV)

A GOSPEL SONG ON WHICH TO MEDITATE: CALLED UNTO HOLINESS

Called unto holiness church of our God, Purchase of Jesus, redeemed by His blood; Called from the world and its idols to flee, Called from the bondage of sin to be free.

Refrain:
"Holiness unto the Lord" is our watchword and song, "Holiness unto the Lord" as we're marching along;

Sing it, shout it, loud and long, "Holiness unto the Lord," now and forever.

"Called unto holiness," children of light, Walking with Jesus in garments of white;

Raiment unsullied, nor tarnished with sin; God's Holy Spirit abiding within.

"Called unto holiness," praise His dear Name! This blessed secret to faith now made plain: Not our own righteousness, but Christ within, Living, and reigning, and saving from sin.

"Called unto holiness," glorious thought! Up from the wilderness wanderings brought,

Out from the shadows and darkness of night, Into the Canaan of perfect delight.

"Called unto holiness," bride of the Lamb, Waiting the Bridegroom's returning again!

Lift up your heads, for the day draweth near, When in His beauty the King shall appear.

This hymn has been called the "unofficial anthem" of the Church of the Nazarene. At one time it was sung at every Nazarene ordination service. It was written by Lelia N. Morris in 1900. Mrs. Morris (1862–1929) was a member of a Methodist church who wrote more than a thousand gospel songs. She was a friend to the camp meeting, and wrote a number of hymns on the message of holy living. When her eyes began to fail in 1913, her son built a twenty-eight-foot blackboard with oversized staff lines, so she could continue composing songs.

A FINAL WORD

It has been the goal of the authors to present the message of the Spirit-filled life in *layman's terms*. By now, it is obvious that the message is multifaceted but not impossible to comprehend. Our greater desire is not only for understanding but also for experience. We strongly believe that it is God's promise and provision for every believer to be filled with the Spirit and to live a holy life. Whether you dot your *i*'s and cross your *t*'s as we do theologically, is not our primary concern. We pray that our study of four-letter words has increased your understanding and experience of the power of the same Spirit that raised Jesus from the dead.

Our greatest hope is that you experience the Holy Spirit in his fullness and daily know the victory that he promises over willful sin, and we underline the word "willful." We will never reach a state of grace wherein we are incapable of sinning. Neither do we have to sin every day in thought, word or deed. The Spirit can enable us with every temptation to find God's way of escape (1 Cor 10:13). We don't have to live in Romans 7. We can know the joy of living in Romans 6 and 8.

If you were to listen to the testimonies of hundreds of Christ-followers, no two of them would be identical. The Holy Spirit makes no carbon copies, and thus, every believer's experience is different. To speak of one or two or even three works of grace seems so unwise. Who can limit God's operation in the life of any believer and who can force upon anyone a pattern that each much experience to be genuine in his experience with God?

However, we do believe that there must come a day in the life of every believer when a definite commitment is made to recognize Jesus as Lord of one's life and begin the pursuit of a holy life. A holy life does not come automatically. We must "purify ourselves from everything that contaminates body and spirit, perfecting holiness out of reverence for God" (2 Cor 7:1), and, "in our hearts set apart Christ as Lord" (1 Pet 3:15).

Perhaps our greatest concern is the weakening influence of the church in today's culture. We recently asked a class of young seminarians in Haiti, "What will it take to evangelize Haiti?" The initial responder spoke wisely, "Haiti will be evangelized when professing Christians live like Christians." We believe the same is true in America and, for that matter, all the countries of the world. To love as Jesus loved could summarize the prescription for an unholy nation to become holy.

The Christian life can and does include spiritual warfare, but it is easier to fight a battle with an enemy without than it is with an enemy within. And when that inner battle is settled, the outer enemy is less a threat. It is also easier to let someone else, more capable than yourself, to fight your battles for you than to fight them for yourself. Few words in scripture are more encouraging than these: "You, dear children, are from God and have overcome them, because the one who is in you is greater than the one who is in the world" (1 John 4:4).

Christ has come to give to us abundant life, not a life of constant struggle but a life of constant peace. Such a life can be found only when we settle the issue of self-centeredness or Christ-centeredness, when we are at peace with God and our will is lost in his.

BIBLIOGRAPHY

Bishop, John. *The Spirit of Christ in Human Relationships*. Grand Rapids: Zondervan, 1968.

Bonhoeffer, Dietrich. *The Cost of Discipleship*. New York: Macmillan, 1968.

———. *Temptation*. New York: MacMillan, 1955.

Brother Lawrence. *The Practice of the Presence of God*. New York: Revel, 1958.

Bruce, F. F. *The Epistles of John*. Grand Rapids: Eerdmans, 1979.

Cockerill, Gareth. *Hebrews: A Commentary for Bible Students*. Wesleyan Bible Commentary. Indianapolis: Wesleyan, 1999.

Donahue, Deirdre. "For Publishers, 'Sell' Is a Four-Letter Word." USA Today, October 26, 2011. http://usatoday30.usatoday.com/LIFE/usaedition/2011–10-27-Profane-book-titles_ST_U.htm.

Dyck, Drew. "Rising Above the Spectacle." *Christianity Today*, October 2014.

Eldredge, John. *The Utter Relief of Holiness: How God's Goodness Frees Us from Everything That Plagues Us*. Nashville: Faithwords, 2013.

Keller, Timothy. *King's Cross: The Story of the World in the Life of Jesus*. New York: Dutton Adult, 2010.

Koehler, Ludwig, and Walter Baumgartner, eds. *The Hebrew and Aramaic Lexicon of the Old Testament*. Leiden: Brill, 1999.

Law, William. *Freedom from a Self-Centered Life: Dying to Self; Selections from the Writings of William Law*. Edited by Andrew Murray. Grand Rapids: Bethany House, 1977.

Luther, Martin. *Lectures on Romans: Glosses and Scholia*. Edited by Hilton C Oswald. Luther's Works 25. St. Louis: Concordia, 1972.

MacDonald, George. *The Heart of George MacDonald: A One-Volume Collection of His Most Important Fiction, Essays, Sermons and Biographical Information*. Vancouver: Regent College Publishing, 2004.

Metaxes, Eric. "Murder, Justice . . . and Forgiveness: The Christian Calling Card." Breakpoint Commentaries. January 29, 2013. https://www.breakpoint.org/bpcommentaries/entry/13/21353.

Muggeridge, Malcolm. *Paul: Envoy Extraordinary*. London: Harper & Row, 1972.

Outler, Albert C. *John Wesley's Sermons: An Anthology*. Nashville: Abingdon, 2010.

Quick, O. C. *Doctrines of the Creed*. New York: Scribner, 1938.

Riley, Pat. *The Winner Within: A Life Plan for Team Players*. New York: Berkley, 1994.

Sangster, W. E. *The Pure in Heart*. London: Epworth, 1954.

Smith, G. T. *Called to Be Saints*. Downers Grove: InterVarsity, 2013.

BIBLIOGRAPHY

Stott, John R. W. *Romans: God's Good News for the World*. Bible Speaks Today. Downers Grove: IVP Academic, 2001.

Vanier, Jean. *Man and Woman He Made Them*. Mahwah: Paulist, 1985.

Wright, N. T. *Following Jesus: Biblical Reflections on Discipleship*. London: Society for Promoting Christian Knowledge, 1994.

Yancey, Philip. *Rumors of Another World: What on Earth Are We Missing?* Grand Rapids: Zondervan, 2003.